MELANIE

*"Whosoever is a little one, let him
come to me."*   —Proverbs 9:4

Maximin Giraud and Melanie Calvat, the two young witnesses of Our Lady's apparition at La Salette, France on September 19, 1846.

MELANIE

AND THE STORY OF OUR LADY OF LA SALETTE

By

Mary Alice Dennis

"But blessed are your eyes, because they see, and your ears, because they hear. For, amen, I say to you, many prophets and just men have desired to see the things that you see, and have not seen them, and to hear the things that you hear and have not heard them."

—Matthew 13:16-17

TAN BOOKS AND PUBLISHERS, INC.
Rockford, Illinois 61105

Library of Congress Catalog Card No.: 95-60488

ISBN: 0-89555-522-0

Printed and bound in the United States of America.

TAN BOOKS AND PUBLISHERS, INC.
P.O. Box 424
Rockford, Illinois 61105

1995

"Come closer, my children. Do not be afraid! I am here to bring you great news."

—Our Lady of La Salette
to Melanie and Maximin
September 19, 1846

CONTENTS

"His appearances became less frequent. But the immense light of the Almighty never ceased. My soul was united to my Beloved, who made Himself at home in my heart as though it were tied by chains. The eye of my soul was riveted on Him to take His orders, to do His good pleasure..."

—Melanie, age 12
(*See p.* 49)

MELANIE

"*And a great sign appeared in heaven: a woman clothed with the sun, and the moon under her feet, and on her head a crown of twelve stars: and being with child, she cried travailing in birth, and was in pain to be delivered.*"

—Apocalypse 12:1-2

Chapter 1

THE CHILD WHO DIDN'T LIKE NOISE

Melanie Calvat was born on November 7, 1831 in the little town of Corps. Corps is a small market town high in the Alps of Dauphiny on the Drac River in southern France. It is twenty-two miles southeast of Grenoble. There is always the sound of running water in Corps. Mountains nine to ten thousand feet high look down on the town. They shelter the little town from the worst of the winter storms.

Melanie was baptized on November 8 and was given the name of Françoise Melanie. But she was always called Melanie. She received a warm welcome, because there were already two older boys, and her parents eagerly desired a little girl. They had had a little girl, but she hadn't stayed. However, this baby was stronger and bigger and they had great hopes that she would live.

The baby lived, but alas, she was a great disappointment right from the start. Julie Calvat, her mother, was gay and sociable; she loved parties and all the town's festivals. She had looked forward to dressing up a pretty little daughter and taking her to all the parties and gatherings.

But as early as six months old this baby showed a great fear of crowds. In a crowd of people the little one would bury her face in her mother's shoulder and scream with terror. Her mother, who loved sociability, thought that she would surely outgrow this fear. But she didn't. Julie Calvat grew more and more impatient with this strange child. By the time Melanie was four years old, this irritation had hardened into a strong dislike.

Melanie was always a quiet child. One of her earliest memories was of her father, Pierre Calvat, picking her up and setting her on his knee. He held a crucifix in his hand. Then he told her about the good Jesus who had died on the Cross in order to save men from their sins. Pierre explained that it was a painful way to die. But the good Jesus had willingly accepted that death because He loved men so much. Melanie was only two or three at the time, but even so she understood what her father was telling her. She always remembered it.

When the crucifix was back on the wall, Melanie would stand in front of it and talk to the good Jesus. But He didn't answer; He was always quiet. So she thought it best if she were quiet, too. She was so quiet in that noisy, busy household that she was known as the "Mute" or the "Silent One."

Pierre Calvat was a stone mason, and he often had a hard time finding work. Sometimes he had to travel a long ways from Corps, and even then he didn't bring home much money. For times were hard. So Julie, pleasure-loving and irresponsible, was often left alone to run her house and cope with her lively brood of children. For more children were born after Melanie.

One day when Melanie was scarcely three years old and Julie found her more than usually trying, she shook the child and said to her,

"You are utterly impossible! I've had enough of you. I will not be mother to a child like you. You are not to call me 'Mama' anymore. You can call me 'Julie.' And I will call you 'Vixen' or 'She-Wolf.'"

Julie took the howling child and shoved her out the back door. "Get out of this house. You can go live in the woods with the foxes and wolves. I will have no more of you. And don't come back!" she yelled.

The woods were not far from the house. Melanie ran down the path a ways into the woods. She sat down under a big oak tree and cried and cried and cried until she fell asleep.

Chapter 2

IN THE WOODS

Melanie slept a long time, and while she slept, she had a strange dream. A little boy about her age came towards her. He was a beautiful child dressed in white. His auburn hair was parted in the middle and hung in waves to his shoulders. His skin was fair and rosy, and his eyes were gentle but very penetrating. He had a wreath of white roses on his head. It was the kind of wreath the children wore for First Communion. Melanie had seen this child before—"nearly every day since I could remember." But this was to be the first time he spoke to her.

"Good morning, sister. Why are you crying?" he asked. "I've come to comfort you."

Melanie replied, "Talk in a low voice. I don't like noise. I'm crying because I would like a mother. I lived in a house with a woman and her children. But this woman doesn't want me anymore. Oh," she sobbed, "if only I had a mother!"

"Sister," said the little boy, "Call me 'Brother.' I am your good brother. I will take care of you. We have a mother."

"A mother! A mother!" cried Melanie, still weeping. "Where is she, Brother, so that I may run quickly and find her?"

"Someday I will take you to see our mother," said the boy. After that he told Melanie about God, His goodness and His power, and the life of His Son Jesus Christ on earth, and of His death on the Cross. While the boy was speaking of Christ's painful death, the little girl said to him, "O Brother, don't tell me any more. I know how much the good Lord suffered to get us to Heaven. The man in the house where I lived told me all about it. I too want to suffer like the good Jesus. Oh, I wouldn't dare enter Heaven if I didn't suffer like the good Lord."

Then her brother held out his hand to her and asked, "Where would you like to go?"

Immediately she answered. "To Calvary."

"Very well," he said, "but be careful to stay close to me, in case you fall."

Then the woods disappeared. They found themselves at the foot of a high mountain and began the difficult ascent. The path that led to the summit was steep and strewn with boulders and briars. The further they went, the larger were the rocks and the longer the thorns. Clouds gathered, the sky darkened, and it began to rain. But it was raining crosses—little crosses and big crosses, crosses of all sizes. The little girl fell, almost buried by the crosses. She cried out for help. Her brother came towards her and said, "We're not there yet. If you want to turn back, you will have less trouble."

"No," she replied. "I want to come with you. I will follow after you, and where you put your foot, I will put mine."

"My sister," he said, "you have guessed the secret!" And he held out his hand which, although small, was very strong. But the climbing was hard and the crosses still fell and were painful as they struck.

In the meantime a wider, easier road went along near them. This road was crowded with people. These people laughed and sang, and when they saw the two children struggling upwards along the rocky path, they taunted them, calling them idiots, madmen and fools. Some of the people were on foot and some were in beautiful carriages. But soon this road went over a cliff and the people were swallowed up in an abyss from which arose clouds of smoke and flames. Terrified, Melanie fell on her knees and offered to suffer each day of her life in reparation for all the outrages committed against God.

Melanie awoke to find herself still under the oak tree, and the sun was just rising. She got up from her bed of leaves feeling very hungry.

Suddenly she heard a voice call out, "Sister!" She turned, and there to her great joy she saw the same little boy, her brother, coming toward her through the trees. As he walked, all the birds in the woods began to sing. The trees were full of their warblings and trillings. Wild flowers sprang up under his feet, so that he was walking on a carpet of flowers. He seemed to bring the springtime with him. He still wore a crown of white roses. Melanie was afraid that he was going to spoil it before his First Communion day arrived.

"Why do you wear a crown of roses?" she asked.

"Because before, I wore another kind," he answered smiling. He carried a lily in his hand.

"Drink!" he said.

She tilted the cup of the blossom he offered her and drank the nectar in it. It was delicious and so strengthening that it satisfied her hunger for several days.

"What favor would you like?" asked her brother after she had fortified herself.

"If it is the wish of Almighty God, I should like to serve Him in the way of the Cross," she answered.

Her brother then blew on her lips, put His hands on her head, His right hand on her right hand, His left hand on her left hand. He touched her feet and then her heart. Melanie suddenly felt pain, sorrowful but loving pain, in all the places that her brother had touched. She could not speak; she felt drowned in this loving pain.

Thus, as a little child, Melanie was given the honor of the Stigmata. From that moment on, she felt pain in the parts of her body that had been touched. Sometimes, particularly on Fridays and during Lent, sores would form and blood would come out. This blood was very displeasing to the child. She who above all wanted to remain unnoticed was made conspicuous.

"Besides," said Melanie, "it's not clean."

So she prayed that the pains would remain with her but that the wounds would not show. However, in solitude, away from everyone, they often bled. Then they would heal of their own accord and not leave even a trace of a scar.

Her brother came to see her every day while she was in the woods; sometimes he appeared several times a day. He would talk about the life of Our Lord Jesus Christ when He was a child at Nazareth. Or, he would talk about Christ's Passion and all the sufferings He went through when captured by the Roman soldiers, until His death on the Cross.

But sometimes the two children would just play as any little children do. Melanie and her brother would see who could stand on one foot the longest; then, putting both feet together, they would see who could jump the highest. Then they would grab each other's hands and pull each other over. Breathless and laughing, they would tumble onto the grass. All that playing made them thirsty, so then they picked the berries that grew wild in the woods.

Melanie wanted to know if she and her brother were the same size.

"I want to measure you against this tree," she said; "then you can measure me."

They measured and found that they were exactly the same size.

"Let's pick some flowers," suggested her brother after that. "We will offer them to the good Lord together along with our hearts."

"Yes, let's see who can pick the most!" cried Melanie.

So they separated, each busily picking flowers. When each had a bunch, Melanie said, "O Brother, where did you find these? Mine aren't nearly as pretty. Tell me, where did you find them? Oh, I want flowers like those to give to the good Lord."

Her brother replied, "Sister of my heart, look: to pick this flower, you have to put yourself level with the ground. We can see it because we are small, and we can pick it easily. Now this one grows tall and its big leaves protect it from the neighboring plants. This one by its whiteness is the queen of the flowers. It is hard to find."

Melanie ran to find the same flowers, but could not. So she wanted to exchange bunches. Her brother agreed. But as soon as they had done so, she said, "No, no, Brother, I can't do that. It's not right. The good Lord who grew them would know that

I didn't pick them."

So her brother gave her back her bouquet. But in his hands, Melanie's flowers had become exactly like his! Together they offered their flowers to God the Father through Jesus Christ.

Another day when her brother came, he was dressed in rose color and wore a wreath of red roses. Melanie was still wearing her blue and white dress.

"Why don't you wear blue as I do?" she asked. "Then we will be just the same."

"Someday," he answered with a smile. "Now let's play 'Hide and Seek.'" And he explained to her how this was played. "At first you draw straws to see who will hide first. I will hide and you will hunt until you have found me. Turn around so you can't see me; put your hands over your eyes."

Then a minute afterwards, he called, "Ready!"

So Melanie turned around and began to hunt behind all the bushes and undergrowth. But she could not find him. Finally, irritated at being all alone, she called out, "Brother, my lovely Brother, where are you?"

But he didn't answer; she had to hunt for him. Then it was her turn. Melanie hid, but he found her right away. She said, "You must have looked. That's not fair."

She hid again. Then he pretended he could not find her, and he hunted and hunted, calling, "Sister, Sister, where is my dear sister?"

Then he found her behind some little trees.

"Ah, there she is!" he exclaimed joyfully.

One happy day after another went by with this beautiful little boy as her friend and playmate. She did not question where he came from or where he went when they parted. She just accepted him as her brother.

"I just took his word that he was my brother and that I was his sister," said Melanie when she was older.

One morning her brother said, "Sister, today we will go to see our mother."

Then began a marvelous voyage. Seated on a carpet of grass and wild flowers, the two children were carried a tremendous distance. They found themselves standing before a large door of dazzling whiteness edged in gold.

"Oh!" cried Melanie, "I will die if this brightness isn't dimmed. Brother, what is this?"

"This," answered her brother, "is the door of my mother's house. Leave behind here all the troubles of the earth. Go in and see."

The big door was opened and the children went in. A crowd of handsome people met them and bowed before Melanie's little brother. Melanie was overwhelmed by the beauty around her. She clung tightly to her brother's hand and followed after him. A group of lovely girls began to sing a song of which the chorus went: "One more sister! One more sister!"

Then Melanie saw a great lady. . .no, a beautiful queen, royally dressed in splendid robes sprinkled with diamonds that dazzled her eyes. She was far more beautiful than anyone else around her. She came down from her throne, stood before Melanie's brother and bowed deeply. Then her brother said to her, "Sister, here is our mother."

Hardly had he spoken when Melanie felt herself drawn to the mother. She ran, still holding her brother by the hand, and threw herself into the arms of her mother, crying, "Mother, Mother! My own Mother!"

"My little daughter, my dear child," said the beautiful lady, "Yes, I am your mother. Be my child and walk in my footsteps. Now come with me." And she took Melanie with her.

Melanie's little brother seemed to have become a great personage, but it was still he. He sat down on a magnificent shining throne at the right of a very high and luminous person whom she assumed to be the Eternal Father. At the left of the Father sat her mother on a throne of shining white decorated with gold. At the right of her brother was a very beautiful and resplendent throne on which sat Saint Joseph. Then Melanie, the little girl who was disliked by her earthly mother, was told by her heavenly mother to sit on a little seat to the left. As she sat there, peace and great happiness flowed over her. Her mother looked at the little brother, and a choir of girls, all with different musical instruments, began to sing and to play so beautifully that it was impossible to describe. This music seemed to go right through Melanie and to strengthen her.

After several days spent in a happiness inexpressible, her little brother took her back to the woods and told her that it was time to go home. The delightful and enchanted holiday had come to an end.

Walking home along the path from the woods, Melanie met her father. He had been hunting for her.

"Where have you been? You have been gone for days! Are you all right?" asked the agitated man.

Melanie had no idea whether she had been gone for a few days or a few weeks.

"Have you had anything to eat?" he asked, bewildered.

"Oh, yes, my brother brought me lots of good things," she said.

And she told her father all about this nice brother who had talked to her and played games with her. This mystified the poor man even further.

Melanie never knew until she was grown up that this wonderful brother of hers, the playmate and teacher of her childhood, was none other than the Christ Child.

Chapter 3

THE SHEPHERDESS

After a short interval of peace following Melanie's return from the woods, life at home became stormy again. The father left to find more work, and Melanie was at the mercy of her mother's temper once more. Often she was made to sleep under her mother's bed. Sometimes she had to spend most of the day there, too. Or she would be chased out of the house and told to lose herself in the woods. This punishment Melanie did not mind, because she was sure to see her little Brother in the woods.

One day, Julie Calvat took Melanie with her to see some neighbors. She thought that if the child saw more people she would get over her abnormal shyness and timidity. At the house there was a group of ladies gathered together sewing. They were making clothes for some dolls.

Melanie sat in a corner, watching quietly. She thought the dolls were very small children. She wanted one because she thought it would love the dear Lord and she could talk to it about God. But how could she get one?

When she was back in her own home by herself, she saw two pennies in a drawer in her mother's bureau. Quickly she took the two pennies, and went to buy a doll at the store. When she got home with it, she set the doll on a chair and began to teach it about God. Then she tried to make it say the holy names of Jesus and Mary.

While she was doing this, her mother returned home and was astonished to hear her silent child talking. She went to see what she was up to. Melanie, seeing her mother, said, "I don't want this doll baby anymore. I don't like her. I can't make her say

Jesus' name."

The mother asked Melanie who had given her the doll.

"Oh, nobody gave the doll baby to me," replied the child inno-
cently. "I saw two pennies in a drawer. So I took them and
bought the baby."

Julie flew into a rage and took the doll from Melanie. She
scolded her severely and said that she was a thief and a disobe-
dient child and would surely end her days in prison.

"God certainly is not pleased with you," she ended.

Melanie said she was sorry. She said she would return the
two pennies. She was sure that she could get two pennies from
her father. But still she was troubled that she had done such
a bad thing. So she prayed that God in the future would let her
see and hear only what was right and that He would let her
know when something was wrong.

Her prayer was heard.

That evening the Calvat family all went to see a magician that
had come to town. Julie Calvat was thrilled and fascinated by
all the amazing things the magician did. The other children were
completely enthralled also. And Julie was pleased to see that
Melanie was sitting there quietly.

"And now, for my final performance," announced the magician, "I am going to cut off a man's head and put it back on
again without harming him. Watch, ladies and gentlemen!"

But at the moment that the man's head was going to be cut
off, Melanie let out a loud cry, "Look, look! It's not true, it's
only a trick. My eyes don't want to look at something wrong."

And the child began to cry so hard that she had to be taken
home. Once home, the mother in a rage put her out of the house
again.

Melanie did not go to the woods this time. For it was a dark
night. So she decided to seek shelter in the church where her
father had taken her once. The evening service had just finished,
and the lamps were still lit. The church was empty except for
one person—her father's sister. This was a devout and pious
woman whom her mother had nicknamed "Aunt Bigoty." She
was making the Stations of the Cross.

Melanie was still upset to think that she was a thief and had offended God. She went over to a side altar where there was a statue of the Blessed Mother with the Infant Jesus on her arm. She knelt and prayed for forgiveness. As she prayed, the statue disappeared and she found herself in front of Mary and the Infant themselves. The Infant Jesus held a little looking glass in His hand. He looked at it, but it was smudged and He could not see His reflection in it. Melanie understood that this little glass was her soul.

"I knelt down," she writes, "and prayed to Mary, Virgin and Mother, to obtain by the merits of the Passion and death of Jesus Christ, and by the merits of His poverty, the pardon of my faults. And I prayed to my gentle Jesus to give me His absolution. He did it with His right hand. Then the Blessed Virgin made a Sign of the Cross with the index finger of her right hand on the looking glass, and it became clear and beautiful again. The Infant Jesus could look at Himself with pleasure now."

One more blessing and a smile from the Infant, and the vision disappeared. Melanie found herself kneeling in front of a statue again. Her aunt had finished her Stations and saw the child. When she heard that the little girl had been driven from the house once more, she took her home with her. Melanie stayed with the kind aunt several months. At the aunt's house, prayers were said every day, and on Sundays they went to hear Mass at Our Lady of Gourmier, a little chapel situated in a gorge of the mountains on the way to La Salette. They walked in procession with a group, saying the Rosary as they went.

The aunt also sent Melanie to school. There she did poorly. She kept to herself and never spoke. Her classmates called her The Mute. One day the teacher gently urged her shy little pupil to tell her why she would not recite her lessons.

"What they say at school isn't as pretty as what you hear in Heaven," explained the child; "and besides, there is noise at school, which I don't like. My Brother told me that I must close my heart to all the noises of the world. He said not to listen to what the world says, not to do what the world does and not to believe what the world believes."

"What is your name, child?" asked the teacher, frowning in bewilderment.

"My Brother always calls me 'Sister'; that is my name," said Melanie. And this is what she called herself until she was quite big.

At six years old, Melanie was already different from other children. Abused and scolded at home, she had become self-effacing and silent. She was what the French call an "enfant martyr." She was gay and talkative only when playing with her Brother in the woods. She had become two children.

The pleasant stay with the aunt ended one Sunday morning. Melanie and her aunt were walking to hear Mass at the little chapel. As the procession went by Melanie's home, Julie Calvat came out, grabbed her daughter by the arm and pulled her into the house, saying, "It's time you came home; that Bigoty is going to make you worse than you already are."

The winter snows melted, the spring came and the mountain people came down to Corps looking for shepherds to take their flocks of cows, sheep and goats to graze in the high alpine pastures. This was the chance for Julie Calvat to be rid of her baffling and infuriating child. An old woman came looking for a child to take care of her flock. She pointed to Pierre as the biggest of the children. But Julie was not going to hire out her sons. She said Melanie was the one for hire. The old woman said she was very small. But Julie was firm.

So Melanie, not quite seven years old, was led away by the hand to live with an old woman who lived in a little cottage outside the town. Even Julie, not a kind-hearted mother, must have felt a pang of remorse as she watched the fragile-looking child taken away to work for her living. Melanie, small for her age, was to take care of the old lady's flock of sheep.

She would arise at daybreak. After a quick breakfast, she would go off by herself with the flock to the high pastures. There she watched over them—she saw that they did not fall over cliffs or into crevasses. She had to guard them from the wolves who were hungry after the long hard winter of the mountains. At noon when she heard the bell of the village church ring the Angelus, she knew that it was time to eat her lunch of bread and cheese that her mistress had given her. Then in the evening the flock was guided back to the owner's paddock for the night, each of them safely accounted for. Quite a job for a little girl only six years old! Yet Melanie gave satisfaction right from the beginning, for every employer asked to have her back the next year.

It was a hard lonely life, out in all weather—heat, cold, sudden rainstorms in summer, unseasonable squalls of snow in the spring or fall. But it just suited this child, who was such a misfit in the everyday world. Melanie loved the quiet and solitude where the only sounds were the murmur of a mountain stream and the tinkle of the sheep bells as the animals cropped the grass.

In the high clear air with the snow-capped mountain peaks standing around like guardians, the noises of the world could not be heard. God was protecting this special child of His. For eight years she lived by herself in the mountain pastures in the spring, summer and fall, tending flocks of sheep and cows. Melanie looked back on these years as the happiest of her life. She always thought of herself as a shepherdess, and she always signed her letters, "Melanie Calvat, Shepherdess of La Salette."

Out in the pastures she saw her little Brother often. He taught her everything she needed to know so as to do her work well. He explained to her how the land was divided up. He told her that she could pasture her sheep in one meadow because it belonged to the village of her mistress, but not in another because that belonged to another village. He explained further how the world was divided into counties, provinces and countries, each governed by kings or elected rulers. She could not understand the teaching of the school mistress, but she grasped immediately the things her Brother told her.

The long days in the mountains were never dull. Some days she and her Brother would pick the bright alpine flowers. And when they had gathered a large quantity, they would choose a pretty spot and build a "Paradise." A Paradise was a little house about two feet high built of stones. It had two stories. The first floor was the shepherd's dwelling. It had three walls. The fourth side was a big doorway because there were no windows. These walls were built of small stones. Then one big flat rock was the ceiling of the first floor.

The second floor was "Paradise." Only two side walls were built on top of the first floor. Front and back were left open, with no walls at all—because, said Melanie, "Paradise is open to all who wish to enter it."

Another large, flat rock was the roof of the second floor. Then they wove garlands of flowers around the roof and covered the floor with all the rest of the flowers as a carpet. This completed the Paradise.

One day when Melanie was by herself as usual, the Angelus rang.

The bell sounded thin and clear as it came up from the valley. The little girl glanced at her flock. They were all grazing peacefully. So she seated herself on a big rock and took her bread and cheese out of the bag to eat her lunch. But she felt eyes upon her. Looking up, she saw a large wolf gazing at her. He was very thin, his ribs showing through his fur. He came up to Melanie and rubbed his head against her knees.

"Why, you're hungry!" she said. So she cut off a piece of bread and gave it to him. He gulped it down gratefully. She looked up again and there were four more thin wolves looking at her expectantly. She cut her bread into pieces and gave it piece by piece to the hungry animals. Then the cheese was divided likewise and given out. After their lunch the wolves did not run off; they stretched out on the grass at Melanie's feet. So she gave them a little sermon, telling them that the food had really come from the good Lord, their Creator, and they must thank Him, not her. Melanie was a bit hungry, but after all, she would have supper that evening, and the wolves would not.

The wolves often came to see her after that. As spring turned into summer, they fattened up, but not off of her flocks. Other flocks were attacked and lambs carried off, but Melanie's flock was never touched. Foxes, rabbits and chamois (the mountain goats) also came to make friends with Melanie. But the wolves remained her favorites.

"Wolves are good beasts," she always said.

Once a mother wolf carried a little cub to Melanie and dropped it at her feet. The baby was limp and ailing. Melanie said a prayer and made the Sign of the Cross over it. Immediately the wolf cub perked up, completely cured, and scampered away with its mother.

When a good-sized group of animals had gathered around Melanie, she would give them a sermon. She would sit on a little knoll or on a large rock, and the animals would sit around listening attentively. Sometimes birds flew down and joined the gathering. All heads would nod devoutly whenever the names of Jesus and Mary were mentioned. After the sermons they would sing hymns. The old hymn, "Taste, fervent souls!" was a great favorite.

Then they would play games. But they all loved processions best. Melanie had made several little crosses. Each cross was put into a hole in the middle of a stick. Then two animals would hold the ends of the stick in their teeth. They had to hold the stick so that the cross was upright. And they had to be careful to keep step with each other. The two best-behaved animals of each kind were given the privilege of carrying the cross.

All the animals obeyed her; she had only to speak to them. But the foxes were mischievous and loved to play tricks. They chewed the ears of the wolves, and one especially naughty fox grabbed a wolf by the tail and pulled him around till he tumbled over. Melanie tried hard to keep her face straight and not smile as she said sternly, "For your penance, you will not be allowed to walk in the procession!"

It took a bit of practice to get everybody in line with crosses upright and walking at the same rate of speed. The birds carried much smaller crosses in their beaks, also two by two. They had to fly very slowly over the line of animals in order not to out-distance them. But what a splendid sight, as beasts and birds wound their way in procession toward the Paradise, higher up the mountain!

One day three large snakes, about four feet long and as thick around as table legs, arrived. A number of smaller snakes trailed after them. The animals all drew back, eyeing the reptiles indignantly. The wolves and the foxes growled.

"I'm sorry," said Melanie, "but you'll have to go home. You can't stay."

As the snakes slithered away through the grass, disappointment showing in every wriggle, Melanie called after them, "It's not your fault; it's because of that one in the Garden of Eden."

Chapter 4

MAURICE

In the winter Melanie went home to her family. Her mother would not let her go to school or to catechism. She said that she needed Melanie to gather wood for the fire. But every spring the little girl went out to service again—once to look after a baby, but usually to take care of sheep or cows.

The spring that she was ten years old, a mountain woman came to Corps to hire a girl to look after a small child while the family worked in the fields, and Melanie was hired. This family was very isolated. The nearest village was called le Serre and belonged to the commune of St. John of the Virtues. It was a good two hours' walk from Corps. The family consisted of the woman who hired Melanie, her daughter about twenty-two years old, a boy of twelve years and the little child. The daughter was the mother of the child.

One day when Melanie was alone in the house minding the baby, some masked men came in demanding money and food. Melanie did not know where the money was kept, but she was only too happy to feed the men. She showed them the quarters of ham hanging from the rafters. She explained how to unhook a quarter and then watched the hungry men carve it up and eat their fill. When the thieves had finished their meal, one of them—with perverse ingratitude—set fire to a bale of hay and threw it in through the door of the house, where it landed in the baby's cradle. Then the men ran off.

Melanie quickly rescued the baby and got the blazing hay out of the house. But the smoke and the smell of burning brought her employers running to see what had happened. When they heard about the robbers and Melanie's assistance, they were furious.

"We left you to protect the house, and here you are helping a bunch of brigands to steal from us!" they cried.

Melanie was stricken. She had thought that she was doing an act of charity; instead, she had committed a great sin. When her little Brother came to see her the next day, she hung her head. She could not face Him. But He only said, "Sister of My heart, peace be with you!"

And peace washed over her soul. Her Brother explained that she had not offended God because her intentions had been right. What counted was honesty of spirit and rightness of will.

Because of Melanie's hard work and devotion to duty, her employers little by little forgot about her helping the robbers to the family larder.

One summer's day, Melanie had been told to take the cows to pasture instead of watching the baby. She was lying face down on the grass praying to God. She was thinking of His infinite mercy. She hoped that she could suffer for all sinners so that they would stop sinning and love only Jesus Christ.

"I seemed to doze," she wrote, "and as though in a dream, I saw my guardian angel, who said to me, 'Sister, come with me, and I will show you the souls that God loves and that love Him, but who cannot rejoice with Him because they are soiled with sin and must be purified. But if you will offer to the Eternal Father the Blood and Passion of Jesus Christ for them, their sins will be washed away and their souls united to God.'

"Suddenly we seemed to fly; and then we descended a long ways; the earth opened and we entered into a dark underground passage. We came to a door. It opened upon a terrifying scene. I saw souls undergoing all kinds of sufferings; the torments of liquid fire mixed with flames, the horrible pains of hunger, thirst and unconquered desires. In all this crowd, among this multitude of souls in the most terrible sufferings, I did not see two whose pains were similar. All the punishments were different, they depended on the malice with which the sin had been committed and the knowledge which the person had of it. This sight was unbearable to me. I prayed—I prayed for all those holy and resigned souls. I asked God by virtue of the Passion and death of Jesus Christ to lessen the sufferings of these souls and to free seventy-two of them for the love of Mary, Virgin and Cooperator in the redemption of the human race.

"At that moment, I saw the angel of God rush up; he held in his hand a chalice filled with the Precious Blood of the Lamb who takes away the sins of the world. He poured a few drops onto the flames, which immediately dwindled in height and in intensity. Then he poured some onto the souls who had been waiting for Christians to pray for them, and thus seventy-two were released to fly to the bosom of God.

"Oh, if only sinners and people consecrated to the service of God could conceive of the searing pains, of the terrible devouring flames lit by divine justice! The senses that have not been curbed in this life have each their own torment. I saw a great number of souls with their mouths full of liquid fire which they had to drink. These were the blasphemers of the holy Name of God, and of the Blessed Sacrament and of Mary Immaculate. Some souls had hands that were like burning torches. They had sinned with their hands. But not all souls were purified by fire. I saw some suffering from listlessness, from apathy and from depression. All sufferings were there in every shape and form. I thought to myself, 'God wants His justice glorified.' "

Then Melanie awoke and found herself on the grass with her cows grazing around her. After that time she tried never to displease her employers, to keep all her senses under the restraint of the presence of Almighty God and to love God for Himself alone. Then she tried in every way possible to give relief to the Poor Souls in Purgatory and to obtain their release. "In my poor way," writes Melanie, "I found some little things for corporal penance. Our merciful Jesus provided the interior sufferings."

These "little things" were blackberry brambles, wild roses and hawthorn branches which she put into her bed! She also made a belt studded with tacks, which she wore for fourteen years.

The months passed, and Melanie was back in the good graces

of her employers. One Sunday the woman even said to some visitors, "This little girl is a saint; there can be no question about it. She prays and works constantly; she never thinks about playing. She is very obedient. Several times she has even asked permission to sleep in the stable—but of course, I would not hear of it."

Winter approached and it was time for Melanie to return home. But her employer wanted to keep her. She went to see Melanie's parents. Her father was away working, but her mother was only too happy to extend Melanie's period of service.

Up in the high mountains, the cold winds were bitter and it snowed so that one could no longer see the roads. Water had to be gotten at a well fifteen minutes' walk from the house. Life was hard in the winter. At that time matches were not known in the country districts. At night the embers in the fireplace were carefully covered with ashes so they would last till morning. But sometimes on bitterly cold nights the embers would go out. This was a disaster, for no one could live in that cold without fire. A burning brand had to be brought from the village in a covered bucket. Sometimes fog covered the mountain so that it was almost impossible to see one's way.

One snowy foggy morning Melanie was carrying the precious fire back from the village. She had strayed from the path several times because of the mist. She was struggling through the snow-drifts in a silent white world when a gust of wind blew the top of the bucket off and extinguished the fire. She was in desperation—she had either to go all the way back to the village, a two hours' walk, or to face her employer's anger when she saw no fire.

Melanie fell to her knees in the snow, calling on God for help. Suddenly she heard croaking, and there out of the mist flew a large crow bearing a flaming brand in his beak. He dropped it into her pail and flew away. Melanie hastened on to the house, "glorifying God and thanking Him for His blessings."

One day a young man arrived at the house. He was young and handsome. His name was Maurice. He smiled at Melanie, and at table put his hand on her knee. She pushed it away. Afterwards in the stable he tried to kiss her. She slapped him as hard as she could. He let her go, saying, "Ha! Your saint isn't as meek as you thought!"

Melanie was scolded and told to apologize. She did so, but said, "Don't try to kiss me again!"

Spring was slow to come that year. The mountains were still covered with snow, and the flocks could not go out to pasture. One morning Melanie's mistress called her to tell her that each day she was to carry lunch to a man that worked in a stone quarry some distance away. She did not have to go into the quarry. The man would watch for her and would come out and take the basket.

"Now," she said, "if anyone on the way asks you who sent this basket, tell them that you know nothing about it."

"No," said Melanie, without thinking, "I have never lied and I would rather die than do so."

"Ah, little one, you haven't learned," said her mistress, "that if you are going to live peacefully in this world, you will have to lie many times. Little lies aren't sins. Your duty is to hide from people what goes on in your mistress's house. I know better than you what religion is. Now take this basket and come back as quickly as you can."

So Melanie went off carrying the basket of lunch. She had to ask her way and go by unfamiliar paths over the mountains. After almost an hour of climbing, she came to the stone quarry. A man came out and walked towards her. It was Maurice!

She was terrified. She called for help to the Blessed Virgin.

"Mother, my Immaculate Mother! Mother all pure and beautiful, save me! I am all yours! I belong to you! Jesus, save me! By the merits of Thy Precious Blood, convert Maurice and save his soul!"

Maurice came near. He said nothing, he lifted his hat respectfully, took the basket and returned to the quarry. That evening he came to the house. Melanie was called and was asked who the lady was who stood beside her when Maurice came to take the basket. Where did she join Melanie? Did Melanie tell the lady anything she should not have? Melanie replied simply that she had been alone the whole time. She had seen no one and spoken to no one.

For quite a while Melanie carried lunch each day to Maurice. And each time, she spoke to him, saying sentences she did not understand, "just like a parrot," said Melanie. "And Maurice wept. Finally, one day he told me that he had decided to mend his life and was going to marry my mistress's daughter. And he did just that. He put his life in good order with God and with his neighbor."

Melanie's mistresses, the mother and daughter, talked happily about the approaching marriage. So everything should have gone smoothly and peacefully. But no, for one evening when Melanie was returning with the cows, the girl's mother accused her of stealing a large sum of money—the marriage dowry of her daughter!

"Unless you return it immediately, I will have you put in prison!" said the angry woman.

"I have not seen your money, let alone taken it," said Melanie.

Then that evening before all the assembled relatives and before Maurice, the mistress again accused Melanie of stealing and demanded that she return the money. Melanie again replied that she had not even seen the money. She said that she would not mind being put in prison, because then she would be following Our Lord in His Passion. This made Maurice's fiancée furious.

"You have a fine religion!" said the girl. "Do you think God is going to forgive you unless you return what is stolen? You are a hypocrite! Your piety is false and your miracles are false."

"What's this about miracles?" asked one of the relatives.

"Yes, I heard about two miracles that the little Sister did," said another relative. "Is there any truth to these stories?"

"Not the least in the world," replied the mistress, "they were perfectly natural things. Once the baby fell into the fire. Its mother, hearing its screams, came running and pulled it out. The child was badly burned, its clothes were in flames. The mother called for help and fainted from the pain in her hands. Sister ran in, picked up the child and removed the burning clothes. She made the Sign of the Cross and said, 'Don't be frightened, it's nothing.' When I picked up the child, every trace of its burns had vanished. Evidently it hadn't been in the fire long enough to hurt it. So there's your miracle!"

Yet she admitted that her daughter's hands had been badly burned.

"Another time," continued the mistress, "I sent Sister to the village to get some bread. She had to wait because the bread was not yet out of the oven. During that time a little girl climbed up a pear tree to pick a pear. The child fell out of the tree and broke her foot—at least so they said. Sister came up to the child and said, 'Don't cry, it's all right. Take off her shoe and sock.'

" 'We can't,' said the parents. They did not dare touch the injured foot.

" 'Let me do it,' said Sister. 'I won't hurt her.' So she took off the shoe and stocking, wiped away the blood, rejoined the broken bones which had come through the skin, while she made the Sign of the Cross on the foot. The child walked away and they all cried, 'Miracle!' "

"The miracle that I want this saint to perform is to return my stolen money!"

"Enough of this!" said Maurice. "Let this poor girl go about her business."

"And I went back to my work," wrote Melanie, "full of joy and consolation. I agreed with what my mistress said. She was right. Only God can do miracles. Even the great saints of Heaven cannot work miracles by their own merit. It is always God alone who does this work. While I was wiping the ashes off this child who was so terribly burned, and while fixing the broken foot, I prayed and invoked the name of Jesus and the virtue of His cross."

Maurice was skeptical about the theft. As Melanie put the cows in the stable one evening, he said to her, "Sister, don't lose your health over these lies and accusations that they're making about you—I don't believe them."

He had hardly finished when the mistress saw them and exclaimed in a fury, "Oh, you little liar! I see you talking to Maurice. You're probably both planning to rob me again. If Maurice wants to marry you instead of my daughter, he is free to do so."

After some time had passed, the mistress seemed more friendly toward Melanie. She talked at table of hiring her the next year, and she began to praise her hard work once again. Then one fall day, as Melanie worked in the garden, she came up to the girl and humbly confessed that she had never lost her money. She had only pretended that it had been stolen in order to see whether Maurice would be willing to marry her daughter without a dowry!

Thus Melanie, at barely eleven years old, had begun to live the theme of her life, "Blessed are they that suffer persecution for justice' sake: for theirs is the kingdom of heaven."

Chapter 5

THE RED WHISTLE

Melanie was brought home once more for the winter. But the understanding was that she was to go back to her employer at St. John of the Virtues in the spring. Melanie's mother was not in the least pleased to see her.

"My mother did not reply to my 'Good Morning' or to my gestures of affection," wrote Melanie in her autobiography. "So I asked her what she wanted me to do. With an irritated air, she answered that she didn't need me.

"'I know, Mother, that you don't need me. But if I do nothing, that would waste the time that the good Lord gave me to earn Paradise.'

"'Oh, bigot!' she said. 'Here you go again, with your good Lord and your Paradise. Get out of my sight! You will make me lose my mind.'

"I didn't insist; I went to my room and thought about my loving Jesus. I asked Him to give me perfect detachment from all passing things and—above all—His true love."

Julie Calvat would not let her daughter do anything in the house; she just kept telling her to get out. So Melanie often went to the church and prayed. She usually went when no one was there.

One day, when Melanie went into the church, she saw at the foot of the main altar a priest who prayed very humbly. She stayed at the back of the church out of respect for this priest, who seemed to be in deep recollection before the Blessed Sacrament. Then—she did not know how—she found herself near the altar and this priest. She saw that his vestments were dirty and torn and ragged. His face was very sorrowful, but serene, humble and resigned. He said to her, "Blessed be the God of justice and of infinite mercy forever! For more than thirty years I have been sentenced to Purgatory for not having celebrated with faith and respect the Holy Sacrifice of the Mass. And for not having taken better care—as was my duty—of the souls entrusted to me. The promise of my liberation has been granted for the day and hour that you will hear Holy Mass for me in reparation for my sinful lukewarmness. I beg you to make thirty-three genuflections for my soul, offering them to the Eternal Father and to the holy name of Jesus Christ and by the merits of His life."

Julie Calvat discovered that Melanie had been going to church, so for three days she refused to let her go out until after the Mass was over. Melanie was frantic with impatience, but hid her feelings as usual and said nothing.

During those three long days that she was not allowed to go to Holy Mass, she did what she could for the deliverance of the soul of the priest. She offered to suffer with merit, united to her loving Jesus, what this holy priest was suffering without any merit. Thus she had to satisfy herself for as long as Our Lord wished.

One day Mass was said at ten o'clock. Her mother, unaware of this, let her go out. She ran to the church, but she did not know the prayers. So she prostrated herself in spirit before the Cross of Calvary during the Sacrifice of the Mass. Then she used the love of her Saviour to offer to the Eternal Father, one by one, all the virtues practiced by Jesus.

After the Mass, she saw the holy priest clad in bright new vestments, sprinkled with stars and shining lights. His soul—transformed, beautiful and resplendent with glory—entered into Heaven.

Pierre Calvat came home for two weeks at Christmas. His wife told him that Melanie had become impossible and that her employer had brought her home because she had behaved so badly. Then she told him that Melanie had stolen a ring from her. Melanie's father was disturbed at these bad reports and scolded her severely about the ring. Poor Melanie was cut to the heart by her father's displeasure. For she loved her father better than anyone else in the world, with the exception of her little Brother. And to be falsely accused of stealing again! But circumstances cleared her.

A few days later, Melanie's employer came down from the mountain and corrected the father's false impression. Then the father himself found the missing ring in a small box in the china cupboard, where it had been mislaid. Pierre Calvat realized that his wife's complaints about Melanie were all false.

"Thus I was deprived of the blessings of humiliation, and as a result my poor mother had to suffer again because of me," wrote Melanie. For her father was furious. He went into such a rage that he threw the frying pan at his wife. She went rushing out of the house with her youngest child clutched in her arms. Mother and baby sought refuge at her parents until her husband's anger subsided.

Melanie was very distressed at being the cause of the family uproar. She brought her mother some food, and all the thanks she received was a hard slap in the face.

"Why doesn't the good Lord let me die when all I do is cause trouble?" thought poor Melanie. Feelings subsided little by little. Her mother returned and the remainder of the father's stay was peaceful.

But when a woman from the village of St. Luce came looking for a shepherdess, Julie Calvat was only too glad to give her Melanie. Never mind that she was already promised to the employer of St. John of the Virtues in the spring. This woman wanted Melanie now, so off she went.

This was a pious family, consisting of father, mother and two girls, of eighteen and twenty. They treated Melanie with kindness and consideration and even allowed her to go to church once a month.

When spring came and the grass was green again in the valley, Melanie took the sheep to pasture. A few days after she started going out with the sheep, she met a group who were also taking their sheep out. They invited her to join her flock with theirs.

The house in Corps where Melanie was born on November 7, 1831. (This is a 19th-century photograph.)

Maximin Giraud and Melanie Calvat, the seers of La Salette. This daguerreotype made in 1847, a year after the Apparition, is the only childhood photograph of the little witnesses. Maximin's sober expression belies his lighthearted nature.

Véritables Portraits.

MAXIMIN.   MÉLANIE.

An engraving patterned after the photo at left. Both children have been given uncharacteristically severe expressions.

The house where Maximin was born in 1835. His mother died when he was small and his stepmother treated him harshly, yet Maximin retained his cheerful disposition and merry heart.

The baptismal font where Melanie and Maximin were baptized. Melanie was baptized the day after her birth.

General view of the town of Corps, home of both Melanie and Maximin. Corps is a small market town on the Drac River in Southeastern France, nestled among the Alps.

The chapel of St. Roch, scene of mystical graces for Melanie, with the town of Corps in the background. This is a view from the entrance to the gorge of La Salette.

Apparition of Our Lady of La Salette in the ravine of La Sézia. The shepherds see the "globe of fire." (Drawing done in 1854.) Note to this drawing: "The artist has exaggerated the size of the rock on which the Virgin is seated."

Our Lady of La Salette. See the handwritten notes by the seers above and below: "This is the most accurate.—Giraud, Maximin" and "This picture is the most accurate that has been made. The headdress is not bad, it is certainly the right shape.—Sister Mary of the Cross, religious (Melanie)."

The shepherds listen to the "beautiful Lady." (Illustration from the book by Marie des Brûlais entitled *The Echo of the Holy Mountain.*)

Our Lady rises toward Heaven. Maximin tries unsuccessfully to grab one of the roses on Our Lady's shoe.

The "Paradise" (little house about 2 feet high) constructed by Melanie and Maximin on September 19, 1846. When the children first caught sight of Our Lady, she was sitting on their Paradise, yet she did not harm it at all.

Melanie has numbered its parts and described these parts, e.g., "1) top of the Paradise, 2) interior and exterior of the Paradise, 3) interior of the little house," etc. One large stone was used for the roof and was covered with garlands of flowers. Melanie ends by saying, "Paradise has only two walls, one on each side, because it is open to all humans who wish to enter."

A sketch of Our Lady weeping, with her head in her hands, as she appeared when the children first caught sight of her.

These statues are at the site of the Apparition. Melanie did not like them; she said they were not exact and did not do justice to the Blessed Virgin.

Ravine of the Apparition. A pilgrim can be seen kneeling near the miraculous spring.

Old prints of Grenoble (*above*), the closest major city to La Salette, and of the Grenoble Stagecoach departing for La Salette (*below*). La Salette is located 22 miles southeast of Grenoble.

Melanie did not want to do this, because her sheep still did not know her well, and she did not know them either. Her refusal annoyed the others. In retaliation, shepherds and shepherdesses both said that if they saw wolves attack her flock, they would not come to her rescue. The shepherds went toward the foot of the mountain.

Melanie liked the heights. She felt closer to God high up on the mountain. The air was so pure and so clear, and she felt far away from the rest of the world. So she went further up the slope toward some woods. There was still snow up there, but there was grass and some of the beautiful yellow rock roses and little alpine herbs that the sheep liked.

A few hours later Melanie heard whistling and shouts and yells from the foot of the mountain. Her frightened sheep came running toward her and huddled around her. She looked all around, and there she saw a wolf coming with its prey in its teeth. Soon afterward she saw another wolf carrying off a little lamb. More and more screams and cries were heard. The villagers had all come out to help the shepherds. Her mistresses had come out too. Toward evening she learned that the wolves had taken five sheep and had killed a dog that had tried to protect the sheep.

Melanie came down from the mountain leading her frightened flock very slowly and gently. From afar her employers saw her and wanted to know how many of her sheep were dead. Without waiting for an answer, they began to scold the child for lack of vigilance, for not having a whistle, and so forth. As soon as she got near to her mistresses, they asked her with great agitation how many sheep the wolves had eaten. She said she was not sure but it seemed to her that they had not taken any. So then they counted the sheep, but they did it so hastily that there always seemed to be some missing. Finally they reached the house. Then they let the sheep in to the stable one by one. Thus, when the employers counted them carefully, they found that there was not a single one missing.

Melanie said, "God be thanked for everything and for everyone forever!"

Although Melanie's little flock had not been touched by the

wolves, still her employers were nervous and worried about the future. The whole village was upset by the attack.

"My master," wrote Melanie, "said that I must be provided with a whistle. My mistresses said that a whistle would not do me any good because I would not use it. But my master insisted that I get a whistle. Confident in my loving Jesus, I promised that I would, even though I did not have a single cent.

"The next morning I was pasturing my sheep very near the village. As I was picking flowers, I found a penny at the base of a plant. My employers let me keep it, and as soon as possible I bought a red whistle made of wood. After that I always went to the pastures with my whistle in my pocket."

One lovely sunny day, Melanie took her flock up to the heights where the flowers were brightest and the herbs were the tastiest. Her sheep were grazing around her when her beloved Brother appeared. She showed Him her new whistle. She whistled a tune, then said, "Listen to me whistle, Brother, and guess what my whistle says."

He answered, smiling, "It said: 'Come, love!' "

"Oh, You guessed. Now try this one," said Melanie. "It's going to say something difficult." And she whistled. "What did it say?"

He answered, "I see My path surrounded with thorns."

"Oh," said Melanie, "You always guess!"

"Now," said her Brother, "it's My turn to make you guess. Give me the whistle. Guess, dear Sister!"

And He whistled, "I hail thee for my Brother, O stainless Blood of the Son of God, precious money for the ransom of sinners."

"Oh, oh!" cried Melanie, "You whistled much too long and I can't guess."

"Ah," said her gentle Brother, "this time I will just whistle a little."

And He whistled, but much louder, while He was laughing, a few short notes: "Stand up, here is the Bridegroom!" "Sister of My Heart, what did the whistle say?"

Melanie, hesitating, said, "Brother, perhaps You said, 'Here is Jesus, and you haven't done anything well.' "

"Oh, no!" Now He was laughing with all His might. "You only got half; you didn't guess it all. It's still My turn." And thus the game continued till He disappeared.

The only person in Melanie's family who took any interest in her and showed her any affection was her father. When Melanie was working with the family at St. Luce, he came home from one of his working trips. As she was not at home, he took the long walk up into the mountains to St. Luce. Melanie was thrilled to see him. He spent most of the day with her. Then Melanie asked her employer if she might walk part of the way back with him.

"Yes, but you must be home by dark," said the kindly woman. "The mountain paths aren't safe after dark."

Melanie went a little further than she intended, because it was so hard to say good-bye to her beloved father. Walking back to St. Luce, she realized that the mountains were turning all rosy pink, as they did when the sun was beginning to set. She hurried a bit.

Suddenly she noticed a boy about her age walking along near her.

"Where did you come from?" Melanie asked him. "I didn't see you join me."

He was a handsome boy, and he smiled as he answered, "I have been with you the whole time."

"No, you haven't," said Melanie very positively. "I didn't see you. You are telling a lie, and I don't want to walk with people who tell lies."

"I am your guardian angel," answered the boy. "I am always with you, but usually you can't see me. I am showing myself now, because you need protection. There is danger ahead."

They walked on a ways, and then they saw two men coming toward them on the path. They were very strange-looking and were waving their arms and talking in loud voices. Perhaps they were drunk, or perhaps they were crazy. When they saw Melanie, they became quiet. They stared at her intently and whispered to each other.

"Let us hasten on our way," said her guardian angel, with his hand on her shoulder. But his voice had deepened, and Melanie saw with surprise that there was a tall young man at her side.

They passed the two strange men with no trouble and walked on in the gathering dusk. When Melanie reached her employers' house, she was "alone" again. At any rate her angel was no longer visible, but she had the comforting feeling that he was near.

Spring turned into summer. Up in the mountains, the summer was warm but never hot. Melanie often worked in her employers' vegetable garden. She liked gardening. One day she had been weeding. She writes, "This work took me straight to God, and I could adore Him and glorify Him quietly. Today I thanked my well-beloved Jesus that my mistresses hadn't yet been displeased with me. Alas! Perhaps my self-esteem wanted me to believe in a victory without battle. Human judgment lulled me to sleep with false success while depriving me of the crosses of Providence.

"While I was working, an old woman going by the garden called me and 'for the love of God' begged me for two leeks for her soup. Quickly and without thinking, I picked a nice bunch of leeks, which I gave her. I was very happy and thought: Well, my dear Jesus is loved in this village. Oh, if they could only love Him as much as they should, as much as He should be loved!

"That evening when I had finished my work, my mistresses were waiting for me. They had learned about my foolishness from the old woman herself who, doubtless out of charity, had told them that I was quite capable of ruining them, especially as it cost me nothing to pick the vegetables. I was severely reprimanded and was not sent to work in the garden again."

Melanie was troubled about this blunder and asked Jesus to pardon her. When she saw her Brother, she told Him about this trouble. He comforted her, but told her that she must always "watch over her heart with prudence."

"Up to this time," she writes, "my dear Brother had helped as though leading me by the hand, all the while instructing me better than the best of teachers, doubtless because He knew me to be the most ignorant of God's creatures.

"His appearances became less frequent. But the immense light of the Almighty never ceased. My soul was united to my Beloved, who made Himself at home in my heart as though it were tied by chains. The eye of my soul was riveted on Him to take His orders, to do His good pleasure. This union with God in my heart gave me an incomparable joy, in which my body also joined, although to an inferior degree.

"I hasten to add that this delight of union with Our Lord does not proceed alone. It does not reside in our hearts without thirst-quenching and salutary suffering. The fidelity of the heart that has God present in it must be above all other fidelities. Because the rule of Divine Love is without mercy. In the union of the soul with the God without stain, all human pleasures, all affections and satisfactions, even the most innocent, must be avoided. Nothing, nothing escapes the Love which is a true sacrificer. It wants the death of all that is not His."

This great happiness of the union with God is what makes Melanie's life understandable. This shy, withdrawn child of twelve carried around within her a secret source of joy, a little hidden fire at which she could warm herself when chilled by her cold, bleak life. All the comforts of childhood were withheld from her—a loving and tender mother, the cheerful companionship of her brothers and sisters, friendships made at school. All these were unknown to her. Her childhood seems incredibly harsh—sent out to work so young, sent out to live with strangers year after year, some of them kind, many of them not. She was often cold in her thin, shabby clothes; she was often soaked by rainstorms; and then, she was often not even given enough to eat.

But although she lacked the bare commonalities of childhood, one must look at what she was given! For mother, she had the Queen of Heaven; for brother, the Christ Child Himself. And in her heart the light of the presence of God always glowed!

She was like a little princess in exile. In her poor thin clothes, she walked the alpine pastures tending her sheep like royalty in disguise.

Chapter 6

THE GOOD YEAR

When Melanie was small, she loved her little Brother so much that she always wanted to kiss Him.

"No," He would say with a smile whenever she tried, "not yet."

As they grew older (the Brother grew along with Melanie), she would sometimes try to catch Him unawares and kiss Him. But He would always duck away laughing.

"Someday," He would promise, "but this is not the right time."

So she had to be content with that.

Melanie was now thirteen and the year was 1845. That year she did not have to hunt for penances. As she put it, "God in His mercy arranged for them Himself." She called 1845 "the Good Year," or the year of graces.

In the spring she was hired by a family from St. Michel, a tiny hamlet in the mountains. This family consisted of father, mother and a small child of two or three. They were poor people, and they had only one bed. They expected Melanie to share the bed with them. She refused, because her Brother had told her firmly that she was never to sleep in the same bed with a man. She did not understand why, but she always obeyed her Brother.

So she sat up the whole night. The second night it was the same thing. Her employers begged her, they pleaded with her. They said that she was making them miserable. She felt bad about that and almost gave in. But she refused again and sat up the whole night in a chair. The third night she was ready to drop with sleep and exhaustion. But she remembered the stories that her Brother had told her about the great Saints who for the love of God had given up their night's sleep. They had even stuck themselves with needles in order to stay awake. Thus passed the third night.

The next day the employers gave in. They gave her a bed to herself. As Melanie described it, "It was a little wooden basin which had been used as a feeding trough for a very small pig." The family had tried to raise this little pig and it had died. The basin was a hollowed-out tree trunk, and was neither wide enough nor long enough for her to lie straight in. With two nails it was fastened to the foot of the bed, and underneath it was held up by two boards. There was no pillow, no sheets, no blankets. In the trough was a bundle of dry thistles. Her bed was thus furnished with these prickly plants.

Melanie writes, "The first night, I lay down without getting undressed. The following nights I just took off some of my clothing. It seemed very consoling to me just to have to cross my arms. The Divine Master was certainly looking after me; I was sure of doing His holy will. I only had to thank Him for the favor He was doing me in giving me a small share in the humiliations and scorn and the scourging suffered by the Son of God."

Melanie slept in the little pig trough for two months. But some other children from Corps were also working at St. Michel. They came to visit her on a holiday and were aghast at seeing the bed she had to sleep in. Soon the neighbors at Corps heard of the way Melanie was being treated and hurried to tell Julie Calvat.

In a few days the little shepherds were back.

"Your mother is ill," they said, "and needs you at home."

Melanie left St. Michel immediately and returned to Corps. When she went into the house, she was astonished to see her mother in good health.

"You will be going to work with another family," her mother told her, giving no other explanation. So she left on Sunday with the new employer, who lived in Quet-en-Beaumont.

As soon as she reached her new place of work, she realized

that the consolation of penances would not be lacking! The name of this family was Le Moine, which means "The Monk." Their name was the only detail in which this family resembled those gentle, pious servants of God!

Melanie's words tell us best what these new patrons were like. "This family was composed of father, mother, a daughter of twenty-five years and a son of twenty-three. After I had greeted my employers and put myself at their service, I went out to the stable to make the acquaintance of my flock. My flock was composed of three cows (a few days later I learned that two of these were bulls) and three or four goats."

Melanie's impression of going into the house of these new patrons was one of blackness, fright and repugnance. She did not know how to explain the anguish, the fear, the interior uneasiness which she could hardly overcome. These people never looked one in the face. Their gaze was always to one side. They looked as though they never washed their faces and hands. They were as dirty as chimney sweeps. Their appearance and their sly looks repelled her. This repulsion caused her great suffering; her spirit felt crucified.

"More and more," wrote Melanie, "I kept my heart in union with my all-good and all-loving Jesus. I wanted to embrace all that He permitted to happen to me."

Trouble began the first night. Here again, it was a question of where to sleep. In this house there were two beds, both in the same room—one, the father and mother slept in, the other belonged to the son and daughter. Melanie refused to sleep in either bed. She told them that she would not sleep in bed with a man.

The patron got out of bed cursing and swearing. He grabbed Melanie, shook her and beat her brutally. But she still would not give in. The second night he beat her again and dragged her around by the hair. His shouts of rage drowned out her screams.

The third night Melanie tells us, "In order that I go to bed, my master began as he had the two preceding days. Only this time he said that he was going to be done with me. He was as furious as his bad cows. I had hardly any hair left on my head; he had beaten me, dragged me around, stomped on me, and he continued to trample on me with his feet, saying that he was going to wipe me out of this world. Wanting to die like a Christian, I gathered what strength I had left to say my profession of faith and to repeat that I would not sleep with his children. Becoming even more furious, he shouted, 'Where is my hatchet? Where is my hatchet? I'm going to cut her head off!' "

All of a sudden, the wild scene in the dirty, disordered house vanished. Instead, Melanie found herself surrounded by dazzling light. Instead of blaspheming, she heard beautiful music, which soothed and healed her broken, battered body. While she listened to this music, her broken bones mended, and her cuts and wounds stopped bleeding and healed over. The music put to sleep all her suffering and left her body sound and healthy once more.

After the music, four beautiful virgins came up to her and each handed her a flower—a daisy, a rose, a violet and a lily. Melanie handed these to her Mother, the Queen of Heaven, who stood near her. Our Lady took them with a smile, laid them against her breast and covered them with her veil. Our Lord Himself held a palm of martyrdom which He said was hers. Although she was still alive, yet she had accepted death for Him. Then this lovely scene disappeared.

"I found myself sitting on the floor beside a broken chair," writes Melanie. "My employers were still in bed. I went out to pray for awhile in the stable."

She found some cold water and tried to wash the blood out of her hair. Her eyelids were all stuck with dried blood also. To continue Melanie's account, "After about an hour, I heard my employers talking and quarreling among themselves." Using all her courage, she went back into the room where they were. She says, "I went in to ask where I should take the animals, and they all talked at once. Finally they scolded me and said that I was either a goblin or a witch. They demanded to know where I had hidden myself, because they had hunted for me through the whole house with a lamp. So I was certainly not in the house, and to get out, I must have gone through the key-hole. Then the man told me to get out of his sight, that I was going to drive him crazy."

Then Melanie went to the stables to get her flock. The most difficult and dangerous part of her work was unhooking and hooking up the big bulls in their stalls. She got them safely unhooked and on the way to the pasture with the cow and the goats. But then she worried all day about how she was going to get them back in their stalls and safely hooked up again. Suddenly she remembered one of her Brother's lessons—Man, before his fall from grace, had been king of all creation, and even the fiercest of beasts had obeyed him. So she said to herself, "Since my loving Jesus has made me a child of God by holy Baptism, and since by His Blood He has washed away all my sins, I can then by the merit of His Blood order my cows to be quiet while I hook them up or unhook them.

"Arriving at the stable, I hooked them up without trouble."

That night Melanie was braced for further battle. But the son had left the house, and he did not return again. So after the daughter had divided the bed down the middle with a board, Melanie consented to sleep in half of it.

After that, all went smoothly through the spring and summer months until harvest time. The whole family then moved out to a cabin in the middle of the field to sleep. They all slept together on the floor of the cabin. But Melanie stretched out on the ground under the stars to sleep.

The next day she was told to glean the ears of corn in her employers' field. When she was finished, M. Le Moine told her that now she was to glean the neighbor's field. Melanie refused; she said she would not steal. This made the man furious. He grabbed a big stone and threw it at her. It hit her in the mouth and broke off her two front teeth. Melanie began to run. But he threw another at her, which hit her in the head and stunned her. If some neighbors had not intervened, he might have killed her. They were amazed that Melanie had stayed all these months with the Le Moines. Normally the little shepherds left after the first two days.

These kind neighbors kept an eye on Melanie to protect her from further violence. They even let her pick the fruits from their orchards, because they knew that she was not getting enough to eat. At the Le Moines she was given little more than pieces of moldy bread.

Melanie suffered another hardship at Quet-en-Beaumont. Her little Brother never came to see her.

"I guess He is afraid of the mean cattle," she thought sadly.

One evening Melanie brought her flock home to the stable as usual. She went to the house, but it was locked up tight. A neighbor called to her that her employers had gone away. Melanie asked where they had gone. The woman shrugged her shoulders. They had gone on a plundering expedition, she said. They often did this, robbing and stealing whatever they could lay their hands on.

Later that evening it began to rain; soon it was pouring hard. Melanie had had no supper. She was afraid to sleep in the stable because of the vicious bulls. So she climbed up the outside stairway and got a little shelter from the roof. But her clothes were soon soaked through. The kind neighbor woman found her huddled at the top of the steps shivering. She brought the child to her own house, gave her dry clothes, fed her and put her to bed.

The next day Melanie was broken out in boils and abscesses. She had the smallpox! Her family was notified, and she was taken home to Corps. Her parents were also given all the facts about the Le Moine family. Fortunately, Pierre Calvat was home, and he said firmly that Melanie was not going back to those people. And furthermore, after eight months with the Le Moines, she was to stay home.

Her father was very anxious for her to make her First Communion. So when Melanie recovered from the smallpox, she was sent to catechism class. But as soon as her father left home again, her mother found reasons why she could not go. Melanie was sent out to get wood now; she missed at least half of the classes. She still could not read, so she could not learn the catechism on the occasions when she did not go to class. Thus, she could never answer any of the questions in class. Finally, the exasperated vicar told her that she would not be able to make her First Communion that year. And she was now fourteen, the oldest in the class!

Melanie was sad and heartsick over this disappointment. But she told God that she knew she did not deserve to receive Him in the Holy Eucharist because of her many faults and imperfections. As she prayed, a voice from within her heart said to her, "Offer My merits with your sufferings to satisfy My justice, and be at peace."

Peace and tranquility swept over her, and she accepted this last deprivation with serenity.

One day Julie Calvat told her large brood of children that she needed some peace and quiet for a change. They were all to go out and let her have the house to herself. Melanie and the four younger children were sent to play near the chapel of St. Roch. This was a lovely little chapel situated outside the town of Corps.

Once there, the younger children ran off to play, Melanie as usual staying alone. She could see the statue of St. Roch through the window of the chapel. She began to pray, asking that she learn to correct her faults so that she would not displease either the good Jesus or her mother. She added five *Gloria Patri's* in thanksgiving for the graces that God had given St. Roch.

Suddenly she heard the voice that she had not heard for so long. It was her beloved Brother!

"My dear Sister, Sister of My Heart, here I am."

Melanie turned quickly around, and there indeed was her little Brother, whom she had missed so much. He looked even more beautiful than she remembered Him, with His auburn curls and rosy cheeks and gentle, penetrating eyes. Those wonderful eyes seemed to look straight into her heart. Melanie thought that perhaps she had done something to displease Our Lord, and that that was why she had not seen Him for so long.

"Not at all!" He said. "In fact, the Almighty Himself sent Me to play with you after your victory."

"Dear Brother," said Melanie, "I don't have a sister named 'Victory.' I have a sister called 'Julie' and one called 'Marie,' but none called 'Victory.' "

Her Brother laughed and then told her what the word meant. Then He said that at St. Michel and at Quet, it had been a great battle against evil, and she had been victorious! After He had explained all this to her, she thanked Him and reminded Him of His promise that she could kiss Him when it was the right time.

"May I kiss You now?" she asked.

With a gentle smile, He told her that she would not kiss Him, but that He would kiss her.

"Oh, hurry, my kind Brother!" said Melanie. "Hurry for the sake of our beloved Jesus Christ!"

Then her Brother kissed her on the forehead, on the lips and on the chest. He blessed her with the Sign of the Cross, and then went away.

The kiss at St. Roch ended the year that Melanie called "the Good Year."

To worldly eyes the appalling stay with the evil Le Moines and the lesser troubles at St. Michel and at catechism class seemed to make this a very bad year. But Melanie did not look at life through worldly eyes. The battles at St. Michel and at Quet brought her great graces. Even the deprivation of her First Communion was accepted as a penance. And penance offered up to God brings down graces. For Melanie the year of 1845 was a year filled to overflowing with graces. Therefore it was a good year.

Chapter 7

THE APPARITION

After the terrible stay with the Le Moines, Melanie was at home for the winter. In the spring of 1846, a man from Ablandins, a very small hamlet high in the mountains of the commune of La Salette, came to Corps looking for a child to look after his herd of cows. Melanie was hired out to him.

The name of the man was Baptiste Pra. His family consisted of himself, his wife and his elderly mother. These were good people who were kind and who treated Melanie with consideration. Later she looked back on the months with the Pras as one of the happiest times of her life. She spent the whole summer with them, taking the cows out to pasture and milking them when they were home again. She was so inured to hardship that by choice she sometimes slept in the stable, and if soaked by the rain, she often did not bother to change her clothes unless told to.

The commune of La Salette was surrounded by gigantic mountains, some of them perpetually snowclad. It was a quiet, solitary life, and Melanie loved it. She loved the cool heights and the fresh mountain smells. And she especially loved the silence, which was broken only by the tinkle of the cowbells and the ripple of little streams, as the four cows grazed peacefully on the fresh green grass of the heights. Melanie also loved the acres of brilliant alpine flowers, which she talked to as though they were small friends. The solitary days were never too long and never dull. This peaceful life was soon to end.

On the 18th of September, 1846 at 11:30 a.m., Melanie started out with her herd for the mountain pastures as usual, when a small boy called to her.

"Hey, little girl, wait for me! I'm supposed to come with you. I come from Corps."

Melanie was so extremely shy that she did not want any strange person coming with her. So she said nothing and hurried on up the mountain. Then she turned and called out, "I don't want anyone with me. I want to stay by myself."

But the boy followed her and said, "Come on, let me go with you. My master said that I was to herd my cows with yours. Anyway, I come from Corps too."

This boy was Maximin Giraud. His father was a cartwright and, although poor, was not as poor as Melanie's father. Maximin had never been hired out, and his father was letting him work as a shepherd for a few days to help out his old friend, Pierre Selme. Pierre Selme's shepherd was ill. Maximin was eleven years old, but was small for his age and rather frightened of the cows. So he wanted company—and help, if necessary. With him was a shaggy little dog that he called "Lou-lou." He said that Lou-lou was a good cow herder, but most of the time she just seemed to frisk around and bark at everything.

Maximin hurried up the mountain after Melanie. She was busy picking flowers and talking to them when he caught up with her. She looked behind her and saw Maximin. She scowled at him. He said, "See, I'm being good!"

So Melanie relented and gave him a smile. He said again that he would be very good and not say a word. He was silent for about thirty seconds and then began to laugh, "Why do you talk to the flowers? They don't have ears. They can't hear you. Let's play a game. Let's do something fun."

Melanie had no idea how to play any games, so she went on picking flowers. Maximin told her that he only had to work as a shepherd for ten days. Tomorrow was his last day, and then he would return to Corps with his father. While he was talking, they heard the clock on the church at La Salette strike twelve. It was the Angelus. Melanie bowed her head and gestured to Maximin. He took his hat off and became quiet.

"Would you like to eat?" asked Melanie after a few minutes of silence.

"Yes," said the boy, "Let's dig in."

The children sat down. Melanie took the provisions from the bag that her mistress had given her. Before starting to cut her small round loaf of bread, she took the point of her knife, made a cross on the bread and then a very small hole. Then she said, "If the devil is inside, let him leave, but if the Lord is inside, let Him stay!"

Then quick as a flash, she covered the little hole with her hand. With a shout of laughter, Maximin gave a kick to the loaf of bread. It flew out of Melanie's hands, rolled down the mountainside and was lost to view.

Fortunately Melanie had another loaf of bread and also some cheese. Maximin also had some food, but gave half of it to Lou-lou. They ate together companionably. Then they played a game that Maximin showed Melanie. When they finished that, Maximin told her that he was still hungry, and of course Lou-lou had eaten a good part of his lunch. Indeed, bread and cheese were not a big lunch for children engaged in the strenuous work of shepherding on the mountainsides. Melanie told Maximin where there was a patch of mountain blueberries growing. So he went off and picked some. He came back after a while with a hat full of berries for her.

In the evening Melanie and Maximin came down the mountain together with their herds. They were friends now, so they planned to meet the next day and watch their cows together.

The next day was the 19th of September. It was a blue, heavenly day, typical of the mountains at this time of year. It was still warm, but with just a little chill in the breeze that blew on their faces. The breeze gave a hint of the winter that would soon be approaching.

Maximin was the same cheerful little chatterbox as yesterday. But Melanie did not mind him now, because she had found that in spite of his jokes and teasing, there was a sweet-tempered innocence about him. He was insatiably curious, asked lots of questions and wanted to know about everything. He played with Lou-lou for a bit, throwing sticks for her to retrieve. Then tiring of that, he began to help Melanie pick "flowers for the good Lord."

When they had picked a large number of brightly colored flowers—yellow rock roses, blue gentians, blue snapdragons, yellow poppies, bluebells, red lychnis and many others—he asked Melanie what she was going to do with such a quantity of flowers.

"We will build a Paradise," she said.

Maximin was always interested in a new project. Melanie took him to where there were quite a lot of stones of all shapes and sizes in a little ravine. Together they built a little house for a tiny shepherd. The top floor had a big flat stone for the roof. This had to be covered with flowers, all the flowers that they had collected. They made garlands and wreaths of flowers, hanging them from the roof, and then the roof itself was covered with flowers. Finally it was finished. They stood back and gazed at their beautiful Paradise with satisfaction. Then they sat down a little ways off and ate their meager lunch of bread and cheese. The day was warm, and the sun, shining from a cloudless sky, made them drowsy. They stretched out on the sweet smelling grass and slept.

Melanie woke up after an hour's nap and didn't see her cows. Calling Maximin, she scrambled up a little hillock. From there she could see all their cows peacefully lying down chewing their cuds. Greatly relieved, she went down the mound again. Maximin climbed up to make sure that his cows were all there too.

Suddenly Melanie saw a light, a light more brilliant than the sun, and she called out, "Maximin—look! Down there!"

Maximin scrambled down the little hillock and said, "What is it? Hold onto your staff! If it tries to do anything to us, I'll give it a whack with my staff."

Melanie in her excitement had dropped the staff she always carried, and a warm and wonderful sensation swept over her. Her heart felt drawn towards this light and she felt a great respect, full of love. Melanie looked at the light and saw inside it another light, like a large globe, even more brilliant. Inside this light was a beautiful Lady sitting on their Paradise. Although she was sitting on it, she did not knock the house down. She did not even crush the flowers.

The Lady held her head in her hands and seemed to be weeping. The two children crossed the little brook and came nearer to her. The Lady got up and turned to them.

"Come closer, my children," she said. "Do not be afraid! I am here to bring you great news."

These sweet and gentle words made Melanie fly to the Lady. Melanie was so entranced by the Lady that her heart desired to attach itself to her forever.

When Melanie and Maximin were near, the Lady started to speak to them. And as she spoke, tears began to flow from her beautiful eyes.

"If my people do not wish to submit themselves, I am forced to let go of the hand of my Son. It is so heavy and weighs me down so much that I can no longer keep hold of it.

"All the time I have suffered for the rest of you![1] If I do not wish my Son to abandon you, I must take it upon myself to pray for this continually. And the rest of you, you think little of this. In vain you will pray, in vain you will act, you will never be able to make up for the trouble I have taken for the rest of you.

"I gave you six days for work, I kept the seventh for myself, and no one wishes to grant it to me.[2] This is what weighs down so much the arm of my Son.

"Those who drive carts cannot speak without putting the Name of my Son in the middle.

"These are the two things which weigh down so much the arm of my Son. If the harvest is spoiled, it is only because of the rest of you. I made you see this last year with the potatoes; you took little account of this. It was on the contrary; when you found bad potatoes, you swore oaths, and you included the Name of my Son. They will continue to go bad, at Christmas there will be none left."

---

1. *"Depuis le temps que je souffre pour vous autres!"*
2. *"Je vous ai donné six jours pour travailler, je me suis réservé le septième, et on ne veut pas me l'accorder."*

At this point Melanie was trying to interpret the word "potatoes" *(pommes de terre)*; she thought it was "apples" *(pommes)*. But the beautiful Lady, reading her thoughts, said,

"You do not understand, my children? I will tell it to you another way." And the Lady continued in the patois or dialect of the district, which was a mixture of French and Italian.

"If the harvest is spoiled, it matters not, except to the rest of you. I made you see this last year with the potatoes, and you took little account of this. It was on the contrary; when you found bad potatoes, you swore oaths, and you included the Name of my Son. They will continue to go bad, and at Christmas, there will be none left.

"If you have wheat, you must not sow it.

"The beasts will eat all that you sow. And all that grows will fall to dust when you thresh it. A great famine will come. Before the famine comes, children under the age of seven will begin to tremble and will die in the arms of those who hold them. The others will do penance through hunger. The nuts will go bad, the grapes will become rotten."

Then the Lady spoke to Maximin alone. Melanie could see her lips moving, but could hear nothing. The Lady was giving Maximin his secret. Then the Lady turned and spoke to Melanie alone. Maximin could not hear her.

"Melanie," began the beautiful Lady, "what I am about to tell you now will not always be a secret. You may make it public in 1858." And then she gave Melanie a long message which was to be kept secret for twelve more years.

Following the Secret, the Lady gave Melanie the Rule for a new religious order. Then she continued speaking to both children:

"If they convert, the stones and rocks will change into wheat, and potatoes will be found sown in the earth.

"Do you say your prayers properly, my children?"

The children both replied, "Oh no, Madame, not much."

"Oh! My children, you must say them, morning and evening. When you can do no more, say a *Pater* and an *Ave Maria;* and when you have the time to do better, you will say more."

"Only a few old women go to Mass; the rest work on Sunday all summer; and in the winter, when they are at loose ends, they only go to Mass to make fun of religion. During Lent, they go to the butcher's like dogs."

The Lady continued, "Have you ever seen any spoiled wheat, my children?"

The children both answered: "Oh no, Madame."

Here the Lady turned to Maximin and said, "But you, my child, you must have seen some once near le Coin, with your father. The farmer said to your father, 'Come and see how my wheat has gone bad!' You went to see. Your father took two or three ears in his hand, rubbed them, and they fell to dust. Then, on your way back, when you were no more than half an hour away from Corps, your father gave you a piece of bread and said, 'Take it, my son, eat this year, for I don't know who will be eating next year if the wheat is spoiled like that.'"

Maximin replied, "It's quite true, Madame, I didn't remember."

The Lady ended her talk in French, using these words: "And so, my children, you will pass this on to all my people."

With that she turned to leave. The two children followed her, drawn by her brilliance, and even more by her kindness. Then, without turning back, the Lady repeated these words: "And so, my children, you will pass this on to all my people."

The Lady walked up the same little hill which Melanie had climbed to look for her cows. The two children watched the Lady's feet glide over the grass. She did not bend a single blade of grass as she walked. Running after her, the two children caught up with her—Melanie in front and Maximin in back. Right there in between them the beautiful Lady arose in the air and stayed a moment suspended between Heaven and earth. She looked up to Heaven, then down at the earth to her right and then to her left. Then she looked at Melanie with such kindness that Melanie felt that the Lady was drawing her inside herself. The Lady's head, her arms, then her whole body merged into the light that enveloped her. Finally the children could just see a globe of light disappearing into the heavens.

While their hearts melted within them, the two children watched the beautiful globe of light disappear gently little by little. With difficulty Melanie took her eyes away from the heavens and said to Maximin, "That must have been the good Lord that my father told me about, or perhaps the Blessed Virgin, or some great saint."

Maximin threw his arms in the air and said, "Oh, if only I had known that!"

Both children were utterly overwhelmed by the beauty and kindness of the Lady. Melanie said afterwards, when writing about the Apparition, "If it had been possible, I would have forgotten my cows, my masters who had hired me, forgotten everything, and would have followed the Lady wherever she was going and would never, never have left her."

Then the children looked for their cows and found them still lying peacefully, chewing their cuds. And the frisky Lou-lou was curled up nearby, sleeping soundly.

Melanie and Maximin returned home a bit early that evening. The two children were so filled with the presence of God that they could say nothing going down the mountain. Even the irrepressible Maximin was silent.

Unnoticed by the children, a little spring had bubbled up just in front of the Paradise, just in front of where the Lady had been sitting. Ever after, this was known as the Miraculous Spring.

When they got back with their cows, Melanie led her animals into the stable, fastened them up and began to milk them as usual. She had not finished when her mistress burst in weeping, saying, "My child, my child, why did you not tell me what happened upon the mountain!"

Melanie replied that she was going to as soon as she had finished her work. In the meantime Maximin, who had found that his masters were still out in the fields, had come to Melanie's mistress, and it was he who had told her about the Apparition. When Melanie came into the house, her mistress said immediately, "Now you tell us everything that you saw."

Melanie began, and halfway through her recital, the son and his helpers came in from the fields. Her mistress, who was still weeping, said to them, "Ah, you want to gather in the wheat tomorrow, which is Sunday! Be very careful. Listen to what happened today to this child and to the Selme's shepherd."

Turning toward Melanie, she said, "Tell them what you have just told me."

So Melanie told the story of the Apparition over again, and when she had finished, her master said, "It was the Blessed Virgin, or at least some great Saint, who has come on behalf of the good Lord. But it's as if the good Lord Himself had spoken. You must do just what this holy one said. How are you going to tell this to everybody?"

Melanie answered, "You must tell me what to do, and I will do it."

Then, looking at his mother and his wife, Baptiste said, "We must think about this."

After supper Maximin and his employers, the Selme family, arrived to talk over the great happening with Melanie and her master and mistresses. They all discussed the Apparition and what must be done.

"How are these children to go all over the world spreading the news that the Blessed Virgin gave them?" said the men.

Then after a moment of silence, Melanie's master said to her and to Maximin, "You know what you must do, my children. Tomorrow morning early, you must both of you go see Monsieur le Curé and tell him what you heard and saw. And he will tell you what to do."

Therefore, on the 20th of September, the day after the Apparition, Melanie and Maximin left their houses very early. When they reached the rectory of La Salette, they knocked on the door. The housekeeper of the parish priest opened the door. Seeing two shabby little urchins standing there, she asked briskly, "What do you want?"

Melanie said to her in French (and she had never spoken French), "We want to talk to Monsieur le Curé."

"And what would the likes of you be telling Monsieur le

Curé?" asked the housekeeper.

"Mademoiselle," said Melanie, "We want to tell him that yesterday we were watching our cows on the mountain of Baisse, and after we had eaten lunch..."

And Melanie, with Maximin's help, told the woman about the beautiful Lady and all that she had told them.

The church clock struck then, the last bell before Mass. Then Abbé Perrin, the Curé of La Salette, burst open the door. He had been listening to their account. He was weeping, he beat his breast and said, "Children, we are lost! The good God is going to punish us. Oh, dear Lord, it was the Blessed Virgin herself that appeared to you!"

And he left for the church to say Mass. The two children did not know what they were supposed to do. Finally Maximin looked at Melanie and the housekeeper and said, "Well, I'm going home to my father in Corps now." And he left.

Melanie had not been told to hurry back to the farm, so she went into the church and knelt down at the back.

After the Gospel, the Abbé Perrin told his congregation about the Apparition on the mountain. He implored them not to work anymore on Sundays, and not to blaspheme anymore. His sobs kept breaking into his speech. The congregation was very moved by his account.

When Melanie went back to the farm, she found that Baptiste Pra had not gone out to work in the fields. The Blessed Virgin had made her first convert.

The mayor of La Salette, Monsieur Peytard, came to the farm to question Melanie. He listened to her account, and he too was convinced that she had really seen the Blessed Virgin.

Melanie continued watching the cows till November 1, the Feast of All Saints. Then she and Maximin were put as boarders in the convent school of Providence in Corps.

A statue of Our Lady of La Salette. Our Lady is shown weeping and holding a crucifix and the instruments of the Passion.

A view of the town of Corps, showing the bridge over the Drac River.

The church of La Salette, with other towns in the background; the site of the Apparition is hidden.

Canon de Brandt, a good and holy priest and a steadfast friend to Melanie. He believed in the Apparition right from the beginning.

Bishop Philibert de Bruillard, who was Bishop of Grenoble (the diocese in which La Salette is situated) at the time of the Apparition. Bishop de Bruillard was a splendid and holy man who, as a young priest, had often risked his life giving the Last Sacraments during the infamous Reign of Terror (1793-1794). After 5 years of investigation, Bishop Bruillard declared the Apparition of La Salette to be authentic; his edict was read from all the pulpits in Grenoble on November 16, 1851. In the following year Bishop Bruillard laid the foundation stone of the sanctuary dedicated to Our Lady of La Salette.

Above: Melanie with several sisters at the Monastery of the Holy Spirit in Messina. She would have been 66 years old at the time of this photo.
Right: Another photo of Melanie.

Très Vénéré Monsieur de la Rive,

Je vous suis très peu connaissante de ce que en ce temps de morte foi, vous avez osé publier le secret dans **Soeur Marie de la Croix** la France Chrétienne, tel NÉE SALVAT que je l'avais publié en 1879 avec l'imprimatur de Mgr. Zola Évêque de Lecce (Italie; et que je l'ai

fait réimprimer cette année à Lyon avant de quitter la France. Je proteste hautement contre un texte différent qu'on oserait publier après ma mort. Je proteste encore contre les très faux dires de tous ceux qui ont osé dire et écrire: 1er que j'ai brodé le secret, 2, contre ceux qui affirment, que la Reine de la Sagesse n'a pas dit de faire passer le secret à tout son peuple. Ce 18 Octobre 1904. Mélanie C. Bergère de la Salette

A letter of Melanie dated about 2 months before her death. In it she protests against a different text of the Secret being published after her death, against the claim that she embroidered the Secret and against those who claim that the Queen of Wisdom did not say to pass the Secret on to all her people. Melanie signed her name as "Melanie C. Shepherdess of La Salette."

Melanie at 72 years of age, about a year before her death.

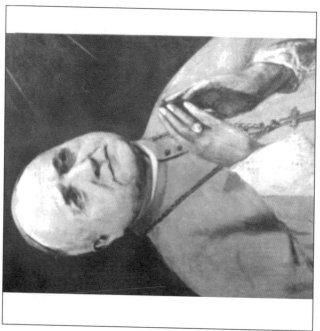

Left: Bishop Zola, Bishop of Lecce (southern Italy), who gave his Imprimatur to the Secret in 1879. *Right:* Bishop Petagna, who watched over Melanie with fatherly care and whom Melanie always referred to as "my good bishop, my holy bishop."

78

Chapter 8

THE PILGRIMS

The children were put into the convent school of the Providence for several reasons. The first reason was to protect them. Maximin, impetuous as always, wanted to rush off to Mens, a nearby town, and convert the Protestants.

"I will get a chair," he told Reverend Mother at the convent, "I will put it on the busiest street corner of Mens, and I will preach to all the people."

"Well, Maximin," said the Reverend Mother with a laugh, "I think you had better stay with us till you are a bit taller. Then you won't have to stand on a chair. In the meantime we will teach you how to read and write."

So Maximin and Melanie spent four years at the school as boarders. Maximin was the only boy at the school, but that did not seem to bother him. He already had an older sister there as a boarder. Melanie's family was far too poor to be able to send a child to a boarding school. In fact, one of Melanie's younger sisters had been seen on the village streets begging.

When the parish priest discovered what desperate circumstances the family was in, the church authorities arranged for the Calvats to receive a small pension. They were never well off, but at least after that the children got enough to eat and never again had to beg for their bread.

Melanie and Maximin were also prepared for their First Communion. It was found that they had never been taught their catechism and knew almost no prayers. In addition the Curé of Corps would not let Melanie make her First Communion until her parents made their Easter duty. They did so, and in time became regular and devout churchgoers.

The news of the Apparition spread across France with incredible rapidity. In 1846 there were no telephones and no telegraphic communications. But even so, in a few months all of France seemed to have heard of the appearance of Our Lady at La Salette. And the pilgrims began arriving in droves. No matter that Corps and La Salette were high up in the Alps of Dauphiny and hard to reach over rough and precipitous roads. This did not stop the pilgrims.

And of course, when they reached their destination, the first people they wanted to see were the two little witnesses. They wanted to question Melanie and Maximin themselves. This was one of the most important reasons why the children were kept at the school. The convent walls and the good nuns sheltered them from the incessant questions of the pilgrims and sightseers.

One of the pilgrims arriving in Corps in 1847 was a young lady named Marie des Brûlais. She came from Brittany, where her family was of the country gentry. Well educated and intellectual, she had started a day school for girls at Nantes. She and her good friend, Sophie Utten, ran a very successful school for several years. But then Marie became ill with hepatitis. Nothing seemed to help her. The barbarous treatments of the day were tried. She was bled several times, and leeches were applied. But nothing helped. She grew weaker and was often in great pain. The doctors said they could do nothing more for her. She was in despair over her health.

But then she happened to hear about the Apparition at La Salette and the Miraculous Spring which had already cured several people.

"I wonder if that miraculous fountain would help me," she wrote to her friend Sophie.

Filled with hope, she decided to go to La Salette. It was a long and exhausting journey for the sick young woman. She arrived on September 9, 1847. A priest friend had arranged for her to stay at the convent school in Corps. One of the nuns was away, and Marie was given her little cell.

There at the school, to her great joy, she met Melanie and Maximin. She grew very fond of the two children and was to become always their supporter and defender.

The morning after her arrival at the convent, Marie des Brûlais hired a mule with a guide to take her up to the Holy Mountain, as it was now called. As they climbed higher and higher on the precipitous path, Marie was awe-struck by the beauty and grandeur of the mountains.

"Do all the inhabitants of Corps believe in the miracle?" Marie asked her guide.

"Yes, Madame," replied the guide. "You couldn't do otherwise, it's too certain."

"Has this part of the country been converted since the Apparition?" asked Marie.

"Indeed, it has!" answered her guide. "No one works on Sunday here anymore. No one!"

"And there is no more swearing?" she continued.

"None, Madame," said her guide. "If someone begins to take the name of the Lord in vain, his companion says, 'Miserable man, don't you remember what the Blessed Virgin said?' And right away the other says, 'Sorry, I forgot!' "

When they reached the place of the Apparition, Marie got off the mule, ran over to the spot where the Blessed Virgin had sat, and kissed the ground. Then she took a glass and filled it full of the water from the miraculous fountain. She drank the pure cold water down in great gulps.

A feeling of peace and happiness overwhelmed her. She forgot her fatigue and her fear of the alarming ride up from Corps. She had been quite despairing about her health. Even her faith in God had dwindled. Now, up in this beautiful and holy place, she was inundated with a love of God and felt her faith renewed.

Her health did not improve immediately. In fact, Marie had several bad days in which she was in great pain and had to stay in her little room. Even so, she decided not to use any of her medicines, but just to put herself into the hands of Our Lady of La Salette. She drank some water from the miraculous fountain every day and sprinkled her painful side with the water.

In six days, on the 15th of September, she found that she was completely cured.

"I am well forever! Glory be to Mary!" she wrote to her friend Sophie.

In thanksgiving, she decided to spend the rest of her life writing about La Salette and the two little witnesses. Melanie said, in her old age in 1904, that of all the books written about La Salette, Marie des Brûlais' book, *The Echo of the Holy Mountain,* was the finest.

Marie kept on with her school in the winter, but she came to La Salette each summer for eight years.. She listened to the constant interrogation of the two children. She was impressed by their courtesy and poise. Even the irresponsible and giddy Maximin was always serious when questioned about the Apparition. The account the children gave never varied. When questioned singly, their accounts never differed from that of the other. There was the ring of truth in their candid and simple answers. Some of the clergy were disagreeable and bullying. It did not matter. The children were always polite. They patiently repeated the account of the Apparition over and over again.

Once a priest said to Melanie, "Don't you get tired of telling people over and over about the Apparition?"

"No, Monsieur," she replied. "Do you get tired of saying Mass over and over?"

As the news of the Apparition spread across France, the pilgrims headed for La Salette. Great numbers came, especially on the anniversary of the Blessed Virgin's appearance.

On the night of September 18 and 19, 1847, 1,200 pilgrims spent the night on the mountain. It rained steadily all that night, yet the crowd stayed there without any shelter at all.

Marie des Brûlais writes that she, the Curé, the nuns and the two little witnesses rose at 5:30 a.m. and walked up to the Holy Mountain. It took them four and a half hours, because the path was so slippery due to the rain.

Marie writes that, to her shame, she had to ride on a mule. The Curé would not hear of her walking that far. After a while they began to meet the other pilgrims. Although soaked to the skin, their faces were joyful and shone with happiness. As they reached the site of the Apparition, although it was now daylight, a dense fog settled over the mountain. But this only intensified the beauty and the mystery. Then two choirs of almost 30,000 voices began singing the *Magnificat*.

The sun broke through the heavy clouds, piercing also the fog. The scene was so majestic and so beautiful, it almost seemed like Judgment Day. The mysterious curtain between Heaven and earth seemed parted, and those on the mountain felt almost as though they had reached the Land of the Blessed.

Two days later, processions came through Corps on the way to La Salette. Whole parishes from nearby towns passed by, led by their curés and carrying their banners. Some had been walking seven hours. And all were fasting. Many had left in the middle of the night in order to be in time for Mass on the mountain. It took thirty-five priests to say Mass for all the pilgrims.

The pilgrims were not just men and women in the prime of life. Not at all! Amongst the pilgrims from Cordéac, indeed walking at the head of the group, was an old man of eighty-two years. Two elderly women were among the tremendous crowd on the mountain. When asked where they came from, they said from Brittany. And they had *walked* to La Salette! They had walked from Couëron, a small town ten miles south of Nantes, all the way to Corps and the Holy Mountain. This was a distance of over 400 miles! They had walked all the way across France! The trip had taken them thirty-one days. And that was not the least of their odyssey. The elder woman, a widow named Joris, sixty-nine years old, had not only walked, but walked barefoot. She had done all this in order to obtain the cure of a young woman she had nursed through the winter months.

Marie des Brûlais was quite shocked by the widow's poor bruised and swollen feet.

"But God does not demand such things of us!" she exclaimed.

"I know, I know!" said Mother Joris. "But I prayed to the Blessed Virgin for the strength to do this, and she gave it to me. We have plenty of money. We left home with ten francs, and still have some left. The Blessed Virgin has guided us, and we have lacked for nothing."

The two brave pilgrims were going home with a quart of water from the Miraculous Spring for the young woman. They had spent three days on the Holy Mountain and were headed home.

"The Blessed Virgin," said Mother Joris, "she is my insurance that we will return safely."

And that was the last that Marie saw of the valiant lady and her friend.

Marie des Brûlais must have been an excellent teacher, because one evening she dressed three dolls to look like Melanie, Maximin and the Blessed Virgin. Then she set them on a table.

Maximin was delighted to see himself in miniature, "Well, look at me!" he cried joyfully. And he grabbed his doll and made it dance around.

"How were you standing, children?" asked Marie. "And show me just what happened."

So Maximin holding his doll and Melanie holding hers and that of the Blessed Virgin re-enacted the whole Apparition for Marie.

Visitors preferred to question Maximin rather than Melanie. For she was quiet and timid and answered as briefly as possible.

Maximin, with his outgoing nature, was easier to question. He was always generous and amiable with the pilgrims and the curious sightseers. One day he had been questioned steadily from six in the morning till ten at night. He was so exhausted that he was almost ill with fatigue.

Marie des Brûlais was sitting on a bench in the room where a crowd of questioners was gathered around Maximin. He managed to slip out of the crowd, sat down by Marie and put his head on her shoulder. There he fell sound asleep. She quickly threw her cloak around him so no one could see him. Sister St. Thecla was sitting at the other end of the bench.

The crowd missed Maximin and began to ask where he had gone. Marie and Sister St. Thecla smiled and said nothing.

The stay at the convent with the gentle, courteous nuns, and no doubt the graces from the Apparition, began to change Melanie's disposition. Before the Apparition she was considered stubborn and sulky. Often she would not answer a question but would just shrug her shoulders. But since the Apparition, everyone noticed a change in her for the better. No matter how irritating or unpleasant the questions, Melanie replied quietly but courteously. She smiled more than she had previously and was far more sweet-tempered.

She and Maximin were extremely different. He was the cheerful little extrovert, and Melanie the silent introvert. Needless to say, they irritated each other, and like children throughout the ages, they squabbled.

"When I'm a priest," said Maximin, "and you come to me in Confession, I will give you an enormous penance."

"Huh," replied Melanie, "nobody's going to go to your confessional. They will find another priest to confess to."

It sounds rather like children of today! The little witnesses were not yet saints.

The pilgrims, especially the women, wanted to know what the Blessed Virgin was wearing when the children saw her. Melanie was the one who best described her clothing. And only Melanie had been able to see her face. Maximin had not. He said that he had been so dazzled by the brilliance surrounding her that he had to keep blinking. Only Melanie saw that Our Lady was weeping.

The pictures of Our Lady of La Salette drawn after Melanie's description show that her costume superficially resembled that of a well-dressed lady of the 1840's. Her skirt was full and came down to her ankles. She wore a kerchief, as did Melanie, which was almost a cape. It crossed in front and was tied in back. She wore a bonnet on her head, not unlike the bonnets that ladies wore in 1846.

In describing Our Lady, Melanie stated repeatedly that her garments, diadem, etc. were made of light and glory, that they were not of this earth, and that they were more brilliant than our poor sun on earth. This must be kept in mind when reading about the particular details of Our Lady's costume. With regard to Our Lady herself, Melanie emphasized the inexpressible goodness and love that radiated from her, as well as her queenly majesty. Melanie felt herself drawn toward Our Lady and "liquefied" by her great beauty, especially by her eyes, which were softness itself yet very penetrating. Melanie wrote, "Our eyes spoke to each other." She wanted to melt herself into the Blessed Virgin Mary.

Our Lady's dress was silver white, brilliant and dazzling. The sleeves were long and wide. They covered the tips of her fingers, rather like those of a nun's habit.

Her apron was the color of brilliant gold and was as long as the hem of her skirt. Her white kerchief was bordered with roses of all colors. Beside the border of roses lay a flat band of gold braid. Then around her neck hung a golden chain which had a crucifix on it, also of gold. Upon the cross were pliers at one end and a hammer at the other end. The figure of Christ on the cross was even more luminous than the cross itself.

The Blessed Virgin wore a high headdress of white, much like the ladies' bonnets of the time. This bonnet had a crown of roses on it. The crown encircled the bonnet, but did not seem to touch it. The roses were small and of all different colors. They kept changing and they shimmered with lights. This made a sparkling diadem of light and color. Our Lady looked every inch a queen.

Her shoes were silvery white with gold buckles. They had a garland of roses around the sole. Her stockings—of which Melanie caught a glimpse as Our Lady was leaving—were gold-colored. The whole outfit was white and gold with the sparkling roses adding extra touches of color.

"Oh, she was so beautiful!" said Melanie. "We never wanted to leave her."

"Oh, how beautiful she was!" echoed Maximin.

"We never wanted to leave her!" they both said again.

Children who are given the extraordinary privilege of seeing the Blessed Virgin do not usually have great worldly happiness when they are grown. Their joys are supernatural. Having been given a glimpse of Heaven, they ever afterward find the world an unsatisfactory place. For the rest of their lives, Melanie and Maximin would be pilgrims on this earth.

Chapter 9

TROUBLES BEGIN

Melanie and Maximin became boarders at the Convent of the Providence for four years. The nuns taught them well. They not only learned to read and write, but they learned their catechism and were made familiar with Holy Scripture and Church history. At the convent they also began to suffer the crosses and contradictions which would mark their lives as grown-ups.

The Church is always very slow to accept any unusual happening as a miracle or as of supernatural origin. Anything unusual has to be investigated carefully and thoroughly.

Therefore, most of the clergy who came to question the children were already prejudiced against the Apparition. Many of them thought that the children were lying and had invented the beautiful Lady who appeared and spoke to them. And they did not believe that the children had any secret messages.

Melanie was asked by a priest: "The Lady gave you a secret and forbade you to tell it. All right, but tell me at least if the secret is about you or another."

Melanie: "Whomever it is about, she forbade me to say."

Priest: "Your secret—is it something that you must do?"

Melanie: "Whether it is something that I must do or not do is no one's business. She forbade us to say."

Priest: "God has revealed your secret to a holy nun, but I would rather that you told me, so that I know that you're not lying."

Melanie: "If a nun knows it, then she can tell you."

Priest: "You must tell your secret to your confessor, because you must not hide anything in confession."

Melanie: "My secret is not a sin. In confession one is only obliged to tell one's sins."

Then to Maximin: "What if you had to tell your secret or die?"

Maximin, with firmness: "I would die. I would not tell it."

Priest: "If the Pope demanded to know your secret, you would have to tell it, because the Pope is more important than the Blessed Virgin."

Maximin: "The Pope more important than the Blessed Virgin! If the Pope does his duty well, he will be a saint. But he will always be less important than the Blessed Virgin."

Priest: "Perhaps the devil told you this secret?"

Maximin: "No, the devil would not wear a crucifix, and would not forbid blaspheming."

Melanie, by herself, to the same question: "The devil can speak well, but I don't think that it was he that would tell secrets like that. He would not forbid swearing, he would not wear a cross, and he would not tell people to go to church."

Father Gerente, chaplain to the Sisters of Providence of Corenc, near Grenoble: "Maximin, I do not want to ask you your secret. It is doubtless about the glory of God and the salvation of souls. This is what you must do: Write your secret in a letter that you will hide. Put it in a desk at the bishop's house. After the death of the bishop and your death, it will be read, and you will have kept your secret."

Maximin: "Someone might be tempted to find my secret. And then, I don't know who would go to this desk." (Then he put his hand on his mouth and on his heart.) "The best desk," he said, "is right here."

Another priest said to Maximin: "You want to be a priest. Very well, tell me your secret, and I will take charge of you. I will write to the bishop, who will arrange for your studies."

Maximin: "If to be a priest I have to tell my secret, then I will never be one."

The Abbé Lagier was very skeptical about the Apparition, but was so impressed by the candor and wisdom of the children's replies that he became convinced that they told the truth.

He asked Melanie, "You don't understand French; you don't go to school. How can you remember what this Lady told you?"

Melanie: "Monsieur, if the Blessed Virgin had told you, you would remember."

And to Maximin: "The Lady fooled you, Maximin. She predicted a famine, and in spite of that the harvest was good."

Maximin: "What does that matter to me? That is not my concern."

Abbé Lagier: "The Lady that you saw is in prison at Grenoble."

Maximin: "Good that they caught her!"

And another time, *Abbé Lagier:* "The Lady that you saw was nothing but a luminous and brilliant cloud."

Maximin: "But a cloud doesn't talk."

Another priest: "You are a little liar. I do not believe you."

Maximin: "What does that matter to me? I am ordered to tell you, not to make you believe."

Still another priest: "Look here, I don't believe you. You lie."

Maximin, with vivacity: "Then why did you come such a long distance to question me?"

The priests were amazed at the wisdom of the children's answers.

One priest said to Melanie: "The devil carried Our Lord to the top of the Temple."

Melanie: "Yes, but that was before He was glorified."

Another priest: "Does your guardian angel know your secret, Melanie?"

Melanie: "Yes, Monsieur."

Priest: "So, there is someone who knows it."

Melanie: "But my guardian angel is not an ordinary person (*du peuple*)."

The priests were very impressed at these answers and found them most astonishing.

But the Abbé Dupanloup was the worst of the clerics. One could almost accuse him of cruelty toward the children. He was a well-educated, intelligent man. He was also a fastidious gentleman who found nothing attractive about the little witnesses. He considered them coarse and crude little peasants.

He invited Maximin to his hotel room, made friends with him and showed him all his things, which the curious child was delighted to see. Then he took a pile of gold pieces and stacked them up on the table.

"These," he told the boy, "can all be yours."

Maximin handled the pieces of gold with delight, stacking them and restacking them in little piles.

"Think of all the nice things that you could buy for your father," continued the Abbé.

Maximin smiled with pleasure.

"There is only one condition," said the Abbé: "that you tell me your secret."

At that Maximin dropped the gold pieces as though they burned him. "Keep your gold pieces," he said, "and I will keep my secret."

Then Maximin left, and Melanie was brought in. She too was shown the gold. And it was offered to her on condition that she tell the Abbé her secret. She was quite unimpressed by the stack of gold pieces.

"But people don't need all that much gold to be happy," she said. No, she certainly was not going to tell her secret, she told the Abbé.

So the Abbé Dupanloup left Corps and the Holy Mountain, defeated by two uneducated peasant children. He would climb in the ranks of the Church's hierarchy. One day he would be Bishop of Orleans. But apparently the Blessed Mother did not like to see her two little witnesses abused like that. Although the Church approved the Apparition, and high and low believed in its authenticity, the Abbé Dupanloup was never able to believe in it. This saddened him greatly. But perhaps it was his punishment.

The Apparition was investigated by the Bishop of Grenoble, since La Salette was in his diocese. This bishop was Monsignor Philibert de Bruillard, a splendid and holy man. As a young priest in Paris, he had gone about in disguise during the Terror, giving final absolution to the aristocrats before they were executed. He would even jump into the tumbrils on the way to the guillotine. He administered Extreme Unction to all who needed it at the risk of his own life.

Now in 1846, this valiant priest was an old man in his eighties. After five years of investigations, he passed on the Apparition and declared it authentic. His edict was signed on September 19, 1851 and read from the pulpit in the whole diocese of Grenoble on November 16, 1851. In May of 1852 Bishop de Bruillard laid the foundation stone of the sanctuary dedicated to Our Lady of La Salette.

The children finally agreed to write out their secrets for the bishop. He promised that they would be sealed unread and taken to the Pope by two trustworthy priests. This was done in 1851. Maximin's secret was just a few paragraphs. But Melanie's was several pages long. In writing it down she asked how to spell certain words—"infallibility" and "Antichrist." The Pope who received the secrets was Pope Pius IX. The messengers noted that the Holy Father was visibly troubled when he read Melanie's secret message.

Melanie was almost eighteen when she decided to become a nun and entered the Sisters of Providence at Corps as a postulant. When her father heard that she wanted to enter religious life, he was furious. He went to the convent and dragged her out forcibly. He said he would kill her first. He actually took a gun and fired it at her. But the bullet went under her arm and did not touch her. Then he shut her in the cellar and said she would stay there without food until she gave in. But after a week, her father gave in. She was his favorite child, and he did not want her to die after all. So he released her.

Melanie took the habit in 1851. For her religious name, she called herself 'Sister Mary of the Cross.' It was a name that suited her well. She was sent to the motherhouse of the order in Corenc near Grenoble.

Melanie's family was far too poor to give the usual dowry for a nun entering the convent. So Monsignor Philibert, the good Bishop of Grenoble, agreed to give the convent a pension for Melanie. He retired soon after, because he was by then eighty-eight years old. This was unfortunate for Melanie and for La Salette.

Bishop Ginoulhiac succeeded him. He was a very different type of man, one whose manner was rigid, proud and authoritarian. He demanded absolute obedience of everyone who worked under him. Many said that he was more like a soldier than a priest. Also, he had political ambitions. He was a friend of Napoleon III, who was climbing to the height of his power, and the Bishop did not want to offend him in any way.

The new bishop was skeptical of the Apparition, although it had been approved by the Church. He went to see Melanie at the convent and asked her to tell him her secret.

"I cannot tell you, I am not allowed to," she answered.

This made the Bishop furious—to be defied by a little shepherdess from the mountains. He left the convent speechless with anger.

"His Excellency will be avenged," said one of the priests who had come with him.

Melanie had to spend a third year as a novice, instead of the usual two years. Her pension was stopped. Then in 1854, on December 16, the Bishop put Melanie in the care of an English priest and shipped her off to England. Bishop Ginoulhiac had rid himself of an irritating nuisance.

This was the beginning of Melanie's wanderings. She was never to be settled again.

Chapter 10

MAXIMIN

While the little witnesses were at the school of the Providence, Maximin wanted to do something spectacular for God. Reverend Mother had told him that he must be older and bigger before he could start preaching to the Protestants.

This was too long to wait. Maximin wanted to do something immediately.

"I want to be a martyr, one like St. Ignatius who was devoured by the lions," he told Melanie.

But there were no lions in Corps. So he and Melanie took the convent cat, and shut it up in a remote unused room of the convent. They brought it no food.

"When it gets very hungry, it will eat you," said Melanie.

But the poor cat, even after several days of fasting, made no attempt to eat Maximin. It just mewed plaintively. The cat eventually died, and Maximin was still uneaten. Death by martyrdom was not for him! The nuns never found out what happened to their cat.

When Melanie went to the convent at Corenc near Grenoble, Maximin was sent to the minor seminary of Grenoble, called the Rondeau. Maximin's next greatest ambition, after martyrdom, was to be a priest. Unfortunately, he didn't do very well at the Rondeau.

After a year, one of his professors said to him, "Maximin, when are you going to settle down and study? You chatter, you are heedless and scatter-brained. You spend your time playing jokes, teasing and tripping people up in the refectory. You don't listen to anyone, and you don't study."

"Next year," Maximin assured his teacher, "I will study. You will see."

But the next year was just the same. His teachers finally decided, to his great sorrow, that Maximin was not suited for the priesthood. They did not send him to the major seminary.

When Maximin was sixteen, a group of men interested in restoring the monarchy to France came to see him. They were sure that his secret had to do with the French royal family. Perhaps it would tell them what had happened to little Louis XVII, who had vanished from sight when his parents were murdered.

These men wanted Maximin to see the Curé d'Ars, an elderly priest with a great reputation for sanctity. Bishop Brouillard was against this plan, but the men paid him no heed. It was said that the Curé d'Ars could see into people's hearts. Therefore they hoped that the Curé could divine what Maximin's secret was.

The Curé was occupied when the gentlemen brought Maximin to see him, so they and Maximin were received by his curate, or assistant, M. Raymond, who did not believe in La Salette. M. Raymond insinuated that the story of La Salette was a lie. Maximin, irritated and tired from the trip, gave his usual answer to those who doubted: "Well, if you like, put it that I have told a lie and have seen nothing." This answer undoubtedly did not make a good impression on M. Raymond, and he reported the conversation to the Curé d'Ars.

Soon after, Maximin had a private interview with the Curé d'Ars. After this interview, the Curé ceased autographing pictures and blessing medals of Our Lady of La Salette. In describing the interview later to Marie des Brûlais, Maximin related that he had admitted to the Curé that he had told lies, but Maximin explained to her, "I meant my little lies to M. le Curé of Corps when I did not wish to tell him where I was going, or when I did not want to learn my lessons."

It seems the Curé d'Ars got the impression that Maximin had lied about the Apparition. The Curé himself would not relate what had been said at the interview, but it became obvious that he no longer believed in La Salette, and it went all over France that one of the witnesses had admitted that the Apparition was a lie.

The Curé d'Ars was in great anguish of mind over what Maximin had told him. For eight years it troubled him. Finally, he asked two specific favors from Our Lady of La Salette. Both were granted. So the Curé d'Ars' peace of mind was restored. He believed in the Apparition once more and he encouraged the pilgrimage to La Salette.

Maximin, like Melanie, had had a hard childhood. His mother had died when he was small. His father had remarried, but the stepmother didn't like Maximin and slapped him and beat him. He was chased out of the house like Melanie. She went to the woods, but Maximin was turned into the streets. As he was cheerful and sociable, he made friends among the other street urchins of Corps. But somehow he kept his purity of heart and his innocence.

The only affection he received was from his father. This cheerful and irresponsible young man spent most of his time in the cabarets and bars of Corps. In fact, Maximin had learned the *Our Father*, the only prayer he knew at the time of the Apparition, while sitting on his father's lap in a cabaret.

His father, however, was converted by the Apparition of La Salette, as were so many in Corps. He became very devout, attended Sunday Mass, and his visits to the pleasure spots of Corps became more and more infrequent. He became ill when Maximin was barely grown and died a holy death.

Maximin was thus left fatherless and with no home at all. His stepmother would not allow him in the house. But then he was befriended by a wealthy couple from Paris named Jourdain. They had come to La Salette as pilgrims. When they met Maximin, they became very fond of him. They gave him a home and then adopted him as their own son.

Maximin had been disappointed at not being able to become a priest, so he decided to be a soldier. And what better kind of soldier to be than a soldier for the Pope! So in 1865, when he was thirty, Maximin became a Papal Zouave.

The Papal Zouaves were a corps of Catholic volunteer soldiers who served in the papal army under this name. They were formed in 1861 to protect the States of the Church, which were being menaced by the new kingdom of Italy. There were five regiments: an Austrian regiment of light infantrymen, a regiment of Swiss soldiers, 3,000 Irish volunteers who called themselves very fittingly "St. Patrick's Battalion," and a squadron of guides and infantrymen from France. These called themselves "Crusaders" and wore large crosses on their breasts.

There is a picture of Maximin in his Zouave uniform. He is rather stout, with a large handlebar moustache. He wears a fez on his head and the baggy red pants of the Zouaves. He does not cut a very military figure. Maximin was in the Zouaves for three years.

The Zouaves were not successful in trying to save the Papal States for the Church. By 1870 the Papal lands had shrunk to Vatican City in Rome, which is their extent today. In 1870 the Papal Zouaves left Italy and went to Paris to defend it during the Franco-Prussian War. Here again they were unsuccessful, and were finally disbanded during the Siege of Paris. But Maximin had left the Zouaves by then and was back in Corps. He was thirty-five in 1870.

Both Maximin and Melanie were never successful in a worldly way. It seemed that everything they tried to do was a failure. But in spite of that, they had been given certain supernatural gifts that the ordinary person did not have. One of these was the gift of prophecy.

In 1870 Maximin was frantically trying to get his adopted parents, the Jourdains, out of Paris. He knew they were in great danger. He sent letter after letter. Madame Jourdain came, then after more urgent messages, Monsieur Jourdain came. He found out afterwards that his train had been the last one allowed out of the city before the arrival of the Prussians.

A few weeks later Maximin said to Madame Jourdain, "Poor mother, your beautiful home on the outskirts of Paris is reduced to rubble. Everything is destroyed."

"Who destroyed it, the Prussians?" she asked.

"No," he said, "it was burned by the Parisian rabble."

It was six months before the Jourdains could get any word

from Paris. But when they did, they found out that Maximin was right. Their home had been burned just when he said, and burned by the Parisians, not the Prussians.

Another prophecy that everyone remembered was made during a conversation with Monsignor Darboy, the Archbishop of Paris. On December 4, 1868, the Archbishop said to Maximin that he did not believe in the Apparition of La Salette.

"Well, Monsignor, since you do not want to believe in La Salette, will you believe me when I tell you that one day you will be shot?"

In 1871, on the way to his execution at the prison of the Roquette, Monsignor Darboy turned to his entourage and said, "Maximin told me that I would be shot."

In spite of these impressive spiritual gifts, most of the clergy treated Maximin with contempt. But the people loved him. His sweet temper, his generosity and his constant kindness endeared him to many. He was always completely detached from the things of the world.

There was something in Maximin that never grew up. His face kept a boyish look, and his eyes were always candid and innocent. He still laughed very spontaneously, and he always loved practical jokes. But the one thing he was serious about was the Apparition.

He had always been frail physically. He had been malnourished as a child and was never strong as a young man. Soldiering had been too hard for him, and he contracted tuberculosis after leaving the Zouaves.

Maximin was very cheerful during his illness. He had not had a successful life. His efforts to be a martyr and a priest had not worked out. And he had been a soldier for only three years. But he did not feel that he was a failure. "The Blessed Virgin wanted me just as I am," he said before he died.

Maximin died a happy and holy death when he was thirty-nine. He is buried, very appropriately, at La Salette. His secret was evidently never meant to be publicized. The copy of his secret that he wrote when a child is still hidden away at the Vatican.

Chapter 11

MELANIE FOLLOWS
THE WAY OF THE CROSS

The English priest, Father Newsham, was delighted to take Melanie to England. He thought that the presence in England of this privileged girl who had actually seen the Blessed Virgin Mary might bring his country back to the Faith. But this was not to be.

Melanie was in England for six years, 1854-1860. Father Newsham brought her to Darlington, Yorkshire, where she was cared for by the Carmelites. Then she joined the Carmelites, making her profession in 1856. These "holy daughters of St. Teresa," as Melanie called them, were very pleased to have her with them. But as year after year went by, and 1858 (the year she could reveal her secret message) came and went, Melanie realized that she was not accomplishing her mission. Her Secret needed to be published, and this was not being done.

When she asked to leave the convent, Melanie found that she was a virtual prisoner. She was not allowed to leave. The nuns were angry that she wanted to leave them, and malicious gossip spread around that she was possessed by the devil. Finally she took to throwing little notes over the wall of the convent garden. These were found and led to her release. But the Bishop of Darlington told Melanie that Bishop Ginoulhiac had written him that if she ever returned to France, she would be excommunicated in his diocese. Nevertheless, with the Bishop's permission Melanie left for France in the company of the convent chaplain and two sisters, setting sail across the English Channel. She wrote later that Pius IX had dispensed her from enclosure, from

Divine Office and from anything else not compatible with her new situation. She finally arrived in Marseille in September of 1860. She was twenty-nine years old by then.

Melanie was received as a boarder at the convent of Our Lady of Compassion in Marseille. This was a school for orphan girls. The school trained them to be domestic servants. When Melanie was first at the convent, she taught catechism to the lay sisters. Then one of the regular teachers became ill, and Melanie was asked to take her place. When the teacher recovered, Melanie was kept on as a teacher. So the mother superior must have thought that Melanie was intelligent and well-educated, in spite of having had only four years of schooling.

Melanie no longer wore a religious habit. She dressed like the other ladies of the time, except that her dress was very plain and sober. It was modeled after the costume she had been shown when receiving the Rule of the Order of the Mother of God.

Melanie always wore a long black dress with a small white collar. She had an ample warm cape, also of black, for chilly weather. And she wore a small bonnet of either black or white according to the season. Her outfit was not stylish, but it was thoroughly suitable and fitted in with the attire of the ladies of the day. Her friend, Canon de Brandt, said that "she could even go fishing in this outfit without attracting attention."

After a year at the Compassion, Melanie and a sister from the convent were sent to the Greek island of Cephalonia, the largest of the Ionian Islands, to work in an orphanage. This orphanage had been neglected and was being run by an Italian priest. The priest had been sentenced to death for murder. But his sentence had been commuted to banishment by Pope Pius IX. He was neither a good priest nor an efficient administrator of the orphanage.

Melanie was only the assistant and the sister was in charge. But the first thing that Melanie did after she had been shown around the orphanage was to take two boards and nail shut the connecting door between the boys' and girls' dormitories. She did this in the middle of the night, just minutes after they arrived!

The two women succeeded after two years in having the badly run orphanage transferred to Corfu. With their work done, they returned to Marseille and the Convent of Our Lady of Compassion. There Melanie tried to get her Secret published, as the Blessed Virgin had instructed her. But the Bishop of Marseille reacted just as had the Bishop of Grenoble. He flew into a fury, scolded and upbraided Melanie, then took the pages on which the Secret was written, crumpled them into a ball and threw them into the fireplace.

As he watched them burn, he said to Melanie, "This is how I will publish your secret!"

Melanie knew then that she would not be able to get the Secret published in France. She said, years later, that if the Apparition of La Salette and its Secret had been accepted by the French clergy, all the miracles that were done at Lourdes would have occurred also at La Salette. Melanie also said that the de-Christianization of France occurred because of the hostility of the bishops towards the appearance of the Blessed Virgin at La Salette.

There was an Italian bishop staying at the Convent of the Compassion. He was Monsignor Petagna, who had been driven into exile by the anti-clerical revolution of Italy. He was the Bishop of Castellamare-di-stabia, a small town near Naples. Melanie was drawn to this priest by his gentle piety and his tender devotion to the Blessed Virgin. He believed in the Apparition of La Salette and was convinced that the Secret should be published.

Melanie could talk to Monsignor Petagna in Italian. She had had no lessons. But from the time of the mission to Cephalonia, she just found that she could speak Italian and could read and write it with ease. Her accent was so pure that even Italians thought that she was from Italy, probably from Tuscany. This infused knowledge was one of the many spiritual gifts that Melanie had been given. As she could speak to him in his own language, Melanie and the gentle old man became friends. She always referred to him as "my good bishop, my holy bishop."

"If it is possible, I will bring you to Italy with me," he said, "for I see that it is impossible for you to remain here."

Melanie a year before her death. The sweetness of expression in this picture makes it one of the best extant photographs of her.

Melanie, photographed without her knowledge on September 18, 1902 at the place of the Apparition.

Anniversary celebration of the Apparition on September 19, 1853. The crosses
mark the path taken by the Holy Virgin as she departed from the ravine.

The Abbé Rigaux, with whom Melanie made a pilgrimage to La Salette in 1903. The Abbé was to have a remarkable dream about Melanie on the night of her death.

The sanctuary of La Salette (altitude approximately 5,900 feet), photographed from Chamoux. In the background is Gargas, at an altitude of approximately 7,200 feet. La Salette, remote and well over a mile high, sometimes looks down on the clouds and can give the visitor an eerie feeling.

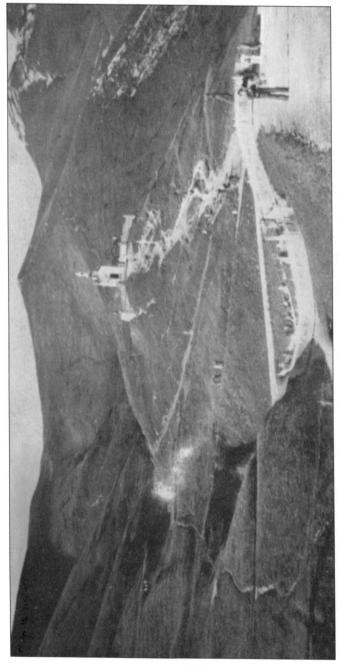

La Salette, with the place of the Apparition enclosed in a white fence. A statue of Our Lady can just barely be seen at the right of the fenced area.

The Basilica of La Salette, situated just a little above the site of the Apparition.

A picture of the Sacred Heart and the instruments of the Passion painted by Melanie. The Latin words say, "Oh, how good and how pleasing it is to dwell in this Heart!"

Melanie holding a crucifix.

The Abbé Combe, a good and holy priest who was Melanie's spiritual director for several years at the end of her life. This office always troubled the Abbé because he realized that Melanie was much holier than he. He felt he had no right to direct her.

Painting representing the death of Melanie on the night of December 14-15, 1904. Melanie died alone, as she had predicted, but the neighbors had reason to believe that Our Lord Himself had come for her. The angel's scroll reads, *Ecce Sponsus venit* ("Behold, the Spouse comes"). (This picture was painted on instructions from Bishop Cecchini of Altamura and Aquaviva.)

A monument at Altamura, Italy in memory of Melanie. It states that she died "in the odor of sanctity" in Altamura on December 14, 1904.

The Bishop returned to his diocese near Naples, even though the revolution was in full swing. Melanie was able to join him in 1867. Shortly after her arrival, Bishop Petagna made a trip to Rome, where he spoke with Pope Pius IX. The Holy Father told the Bishop that Melanie must not live in a cloistered convent but must be free to fulfill her mission.

Melanie stayed there for the next seventeen years. Bishop Petagna installed her on the ground floor of a large villa—the Palazzo Ruffo, with the approval of the Holy Father. The villa was on the Bay of Naples facing Mt. Vesuvius. It had one of the most beautiful views in Italy. There was a room for Melanie to work in, to write her many letters, and a small chapel where she could pray and attend Mass every morning. The country was beautiful and the climate delightful.

Bishop Petagna watched over Melanie with fatherly care. He told everyone that it was Our Lord Himself who had sent Sister Mary of the Cross to them. He was convinced that she was a saint. Those seventeen years were some of Melanie's happiest and most peaceful years. She loved living in Italy. "Most of the people are poor and uneducated, but they love God," she said.

In 1871 Melanie made a short trip back to France. She went to Corps and made a pilgrimage to La Salette. There she was distressed to see that the new bishop, Bishop Fava, had installed priests and nuns at La Salette, but they were not following the rule that the Blessed Virgin had given her. They were living according to a rule that the bishop had made for them. She returned from France distressed at the state of religion there and the increasing lack of piety. She agonized over the spiritual state of France like a mother agonizing over a wayward child.

Back in Italy, Melanie was constantly preoccupied with trying to publish her Secret. Bishop Petagna was going to publish it, but his death prevented it. Then Bishop Zola, another good and holy Bishop, followed Bishop Petagna. He became Bishop of Lecce, a small town in southern Italy. He was convinced of the importance of the Apparition and of the Secret.

Pope Leo XIII sent for Melanie. He wanted her to return to France and establish the Rule of the Order of the Mother of

God at La Salette.

"Holy Father," said Melanie, "the Bishop of Grenoble will not allow me to establish that rule. He has installed his own rule."

The Pope shook his head sadly. He could not exert his will in France. The French bishops were not an obedient lot; it was said that they were on the verge of schism.

As Melanie was leaving the Pope's chambers, one of the cardinals that had been at the interview said to her, "I hope that you have broad shoulders, because when the Secret is published, the whole of France will fall on them."

"I would rather displease the French than Almighty God," replied Melanie.

In the Secret Message the Blessed Virgin complained bitterly about the clergy and religious and the lax and worldly life that they led. Grave evils and dire chastisements were predicted.

The Secret was finally published in 1879 at Lecce under the Imprimatur of Bishop Zola. The Roman cardinal had been right. A storm of criticism descended upon Melanie. She was accused of lying, of being unbalanced, even crazy, and of being possessed by the devil. From then on, whenever she was in France, the French bishops thwarted her in anything she tried to do.

She had picked a fine man, Canon de Brandt, to be the superior of the Order of the Mother of God. But it was useless. Everything they tried to do was checked. Melanie had been right when she told Pope Leo XIII that she would not be allowed to start the Order.

Melanie said that, according to the spirit of the Rule, the Order was to be answerable directly to the Pope, who was its true superior after the Blessed Virgin. The priests of the Order were to be called the Apostles of the Last Days.

According to the Abbé Gouin, Melanie's biographer, Melanie considered the Rule of the Order of the Mother of God to be less of an actual ruling or code than the renewal of the true Christian spirit for everyone. Priests, religious, and lay persons devoted to the salvation of souls were to receive new life from the Rule. Melanie herself joined the Third Order of St. Dominic, probably around 1880. She felt that its observances were perfectly in harmony with those of the Rule.

In 1884 she received a letter from Corps saying that her mother, now an old woman of 80, was ill and practically destitute. So she decided that she must return home and take care of her mother. This was the mother who had abused her so as a child. But Melanie held no grudges in her heart. A heart so filled with the love of God had no room in it for anger. She hastened back to France and to Corps.

It was winter, and the snow in Corps isolated them from the rest of the world. Her mother complained constantly of the cold. She said that if she could only get to the south—Marseille, perhaps—she would be all right. Therefore, as soon as it was possible, Melanie took her mother to the south of France. Even small places in Marseille were expensive, so Melanie went to nearby Cannes. There they found a small, simple little house.

Melanie's sister Julie—the mother's favorite child—lived in Marseille. She was married to a young man named Rémy Oddoc. Julie suggested that the four of them live together and share expenses. It turned out to be a disastrous arrangement. Rémy was a day laborer who was illegitimate and had grown up in the streets of Marseille. The only profession that he knew was crime. He was usually out of work, contributed nothing in the way of money toward the household and abused his wife into the bargain. All three women were afraid of him.

Rémy Oddoc had a ready tongue. He told Melanie that Almighty God would be angry with her because she ate so little. Food, he said, was meant to be eaten. This is the first hint we have that Melanie was now living only on the Holy Eucharist, which she received as often as she could, though the church was quite distant.

Julie Oddoc suffered from severe indigestion. No food seemed to agree with her. One day Melanie found a letter on the floor. It was addressed to Rémy from a woman. In it the woman said, "I saw your wretched wife at the market yesterday. You must make the poison you are giving her stronger. Double the dosage!"

This was the cause of Julie's continual indigestion and ill health! Melanie wrote to the Canon de Brandt, a steadfast friend, asking him to pray for the conversion and death of an "unfortunate person." We don't know whether the wicked Rémy was ever converted, but Julie Oddoc was a widow by 1900. So presumably the second part of their prayers had been answered.

Life on the Riviera was one misery after another for Melanie. One day when she was praying in her room, there came a hail of rocks and green oranges against the window. The window was broken, and poor Madame Calvat was terrified. Some bad little boys had been entertaining themselves.

Melanie was not frightened. Instead, she thought how easy a martyr's death would be compared to the life that she was now enduring.

In 1889 Madame Calvat died. When Melanie had been a child, her mother could not bear the sight of her. But as a sick old woman, she would not let Melanie leave her for a minute. She was completely dependent on her. Although she had never been devout, she did die the death of a good Catholic.

"She went to meet Our Lord armed with all the necessary Sacraments of the Church," wrote Melanie in one of her many letters.

When dying, Madame Calvat asked Melanie to look after Pierre, Melanie's eldest brother. Pierre had become completely deaf and could no longer earn his living. Melanie took care of him for a few years, then found a place for him with the Little Sisters of the Poor. In the meantime, she was in great distress over reports that Auguste, the brother nearest her in age, was leading a "scandalous life" in Paris. One wonders just what this "scandalous life" was. Melanie did not say. Melanie's family were never of any comfort to her. She comforted *them* and sustained them. It was always that way.

After more futile struggles to install Canon de Brandt as head of the Order of the Rule of the Mother of God, Melanie desisted. She had been invited back to Italy by Monsignor Zola. So she sold all her personal possessions, furniture and so on. They brought her less than fifty francs! Then she left Marseille in

August of 1892. She was glad to get back to her beloved Italy.

Melanie went straight to Lecce, where she had been before. A friend of Bishop Zola had found a place for her in the very small town of San Pietro. It lay between Lecce and Otranto, in the heel of the boot of Italy.

Melanie thought that the little town probably had not changed since the time of Christ. The wells had brackish water in them. The cisterns swarmed with little insects, "red as Freemasons," to quote Melanie. The only bread was baked from yellow semolina. It was so hot in August that everyone slept from noon to five in the afternoon. But Melanie was warmly welcomed and treated with great kindness by the local clergy.

Melanie was never able to stay anywhere for long. She was still trying to get the Rule of the Mother of God established. It was a long drawn-out battle between the forces of good— Melanie and her loyal helpers—and the forces of evil, principally represented by the bishops of France.

There was now new hope. Melanie had been left a chapel for the Order of the Mother of God in Chalon-sur-Saone in France. So after a year she left San Pietro and returned to France. Then came more wanderings. The chapel in Chalon was taken away, and Melanie became involved in complicated legal proceedings. She lost the case. Then came trips to Renneport, Amiens, back to Italy, Galatina, then Chalon again, Dijon, Paris, then Italy— Messina in southern Italy, Moncalieri in northern Italy. It is a long tedious list, tiring to read about, let alone to travel. And most of these places represented disappointments.

Melanie had become an old lady by then. She suffered from terrible pains in her arms—some form of arthritis, probably. Her vision had become cloudy. She had a cataract in her right eye. Her health in general had deteriorated and she had become very frail.

She finally gave up the struggle to get the Rule of the Order of the Mother of God established. This and the Apostles of the Last Days would have to wait for another time.

"The Blessed Virgin knows that I have done everything I could, and so I am at peace," said Melanie.

Chapter 12

MELANIE AND THE ABBÉ COMBE

The Abbé Combe had been writing to Melanie for some years, urging her to return to France. Finally she did return and went to St. Pourçain for awhile. Her sister Julie Oddoc, now a widow, came to St. Pourçain and lived with her.

Julie made life miserable for Melanie. She told the neighbors that Melanie was a pious hypocrite and just pretended to be holy. She chattered all the time. She was exactly like her mother. She wanted constant entertainment and was cross because Melanie would not go to the theater with her.

Their mother had not been able to read. But Julie had been to school, so she could read. She read all Melanie's letters and everything that she could get her hands on. Melanie finally had to do all her letter writing late at night, after Julie had gone to bed.

After a year the little house at St. Pourçain was sold. The two ladies had to find somewhere else to live. Julie was happy to leave. She said St. Pourçain was a boring town. Thus Melanie was able to live peacefully by herself once more.

The Abbé Combe was the parish priest at Diou, not too far away. He invited Melanie to Diou. He had found a suitable little house near the church with the privacy that she always wanted.

After sending her the money for her ticket, Abbé Combe went to meet the train, but he found that Melanie was not on it. He wrote to her inquiring why she had not come. She wrote back that she had spent the train fare at the local orphanage. The orphans needed new clothing. More money was sent. This time Melanie arrived when she said she would. Those who had to deal with Melanie found this complete lack of materialism or practicality very irritating.

The Abbé Combe was a scholarly man. He was a fine theologian and mathematician. But one gets the impression that he was not too good with people and was not too well suited to be a parish priest. Melanie in her letters to him sometimes wrote, "Do not be brusque with your parishioners. Treat them gently. Listen to them."

Melanie lived in Diou from 1901 to 1903. She was not happy there. The countryside was flat and without charm. The winters were chill and raw. The cold bothered her now. But what troubled her the most, she said, was the air. She said that the air was foul with sin. She also felt that people stared at her. Now she called herself "Madame Bernaud," using her mother's maiden name, to hide her identity. The neighbors, of course, thought her extreme desire for privacy very odd. She had been so harrassed and persecuted that she had become supersensitive, almost paranoid about her privacy. She wanted no one in her house or even looking into her little garden.

The Abbé Combe became Melanie's spiritual director. He found this position troubling because he felt so inferior to her. She obeyed him implicitly because he was her director. So the Abbé used his authority to ask her questions about her spiritual gifts. Melanie found this invasion of her inner privacy distressing.

He learned something of her extraordinary mortifications. She slept only three hours a night. And those three hours were spent sleeping on the floor fully clad. Her only solid food was the Eucharist. She drank very little. Once she did not drink water for six months as a penance! On Christmas Day she celebrated by eating half an egg.

Melanie attended Mass and received Holy Communion every day. When Melanie did not appear at Mass for several days, the Abbé Combe became worried. He thought she must be ill. He had a key to her house, so he let himself into the front hall. There, in front of him on a chair, was some linen spotted with blood. That was the reason that she had not been to church.

Her stigmata had been bleeding. The Abbé called, "Sister!" and Melanie (or Sister Mary) appeared, looking startled. She whisked away the stained linen, hoping that the Abbé had seen nothing unusual. Normally her stigmata did not bleed, but she admitted that the pains were always with her.

Another of Melanie's spiritual gifts was the gift of prophecy. She told Abbé Combe that all the European heads of state then alive would be assassinated. None would die natural deaths. She saw their murders in great detail. Melanie recounted all this in 1902.

The King of Spain would be shot from ten feet away.

The King of the Belgians would be killed with a sword.

The King of Italy would be poisoned with a slow poison, but he would be finished off with a pistol shot. Then Italy would become a republic.

The Emperor of Russia, Nicholas II, would die of a slow poison, already begun. His father had died that way too.

The Emperor of Austria would be killed by a blade longer than a dagger, but shorter than a sword.

The Emperor of Germany would be shot.

Queen Victoria, whom all will think died of old age, would also be murdered. She would die from a slow poison put in her tea.

"This great evil will continue until the triumph of the Church," said Melanie.

She foresaw her own death too. On one occasion, after having been ill, Melanie was walking in the garden leaning on the arm of the Abbé Combe's housekeeper. The housekeeper, a kindly woman, said to Melanie, "I am keeping your key. We don't want you shut up here all by yourself with no one able to reach you. Why, you might die here all alone!"

"But," said Melanie, laughing, "that's exactly how I will die. But I won't die here. No, I will die far away from here in another country."

Melanie had brought a little chair with her when she came to Diou. She set it in her office where she wrote her letters. When questioned about it by the Abbé, her face lit up and she joyfully explained that it was for her Little Brother.

"The one you played with as a child?" asked the priest.

"Yes, yes, the same one," said Melanie. "I turn around, and there He is, sitting in His chair. He holds out His little arms and He is always laughing. We sit in our chairs and chat."

"Is He a pretty child?" asked the Abbé.

"He is adorable!" said Melanie, her face shining with happiness. "You would want to eat Him up!"

"I wish you would bring Him to see me," said the Abbé Combe.

"I would like to. You could bless Him," said Melanie.

"Me, bless the Christ Child!" The good priest was shocked. "What are you thinking of!"

"But He would be very pleased," said Melanie with a smile.

Melanie could see the souls who were in Purgatory. She had been present during the last illness of the Abbé Combe's father. He died a holy death, undergoing the sufferings of his illness with great patience. However, he had been a careless Catholic for many years before, not bothering with Sunday Mass nor even making his Easter duty.

Melanie was in the room praying. At the moment of death, she got up and hurriedly left the room.

"Why did you leave?" asked the Abbé.

"The judgment always frightens me," she said.

"But he did die a holy death," said the Abbé.

"Yes, yes, he died the death of a saint," replied Melanie.

"But he will be in Purgatory even so?" asked the Abbé.

"I'm afraid so," answered Melanie.

"For years and years?" asked the distressed Abbé.

"For fifteen months he will be in the liquid fire," she answered.

The Abbé said Masses for his father and Melanie prayed for him a great deal. After a year, the Abbé asked Melanie if his father was to go to Heaven soon.

"In three more months," replied Melanie. "A few days before the 4th of July he will be released from his punishment."

One morning in early July, as Melanie was getting ready to go out, she was in the front hall putting on her bonnet. She heard herself called: "Sister!"

She turned around. It was Mr. Combe. He said to her, "I am now going to Heaven. Thank you for your prayers."

The clock struck as they were talking. Mr. Combe said to her, "I am leaving you now," and he vanished upward like a flash of lightning.

When the Abbé was told of this, he asked in great excitement, "How did he look? What was he wearing?"

Melanie said, "He looked about thirty-five years old, majestic as a patriarch. He was as luminous as the sun."

"And what was he wearing?" the excited priest asked again.

"He wore a long white gown with a belt of gold. He had a golden chain around his neck and a diadem on his head."

Melanie went away for several weeks, then returned to find the Abbé quite ill. He was suffering from severe gastroenteritis, could eat almost nothing and was in great pain. He was in bed and said to Melanie, "I am dying. In three months I will no longer be here."

"No, no," said Melanie in a motherly tone, "you are not dying. In fact, you will live to be old."

The next day when Melanie returned to the rectory, the Abbé Combe met her at the door fully clad. "I am well!" he said, "I am completely recovered. What did you do?"

"I," said Melanie, "I did nothing."

"You did!" persisted the Abbé. "I was very ill, and now—just like that—I am well. You performed a miracle!"

"No," said Melanie, "only God can perform miracles."

"But what did you say?" asked the Abbé. "You said something."

"Well," said Melanie, smiling, "I said"—and here she used the affectionate tone of the spoiled child—" 'Madonna mia, the Father is sick. He works for you. And you have left him like this!' That is all."

That had been enough. The Father was well again. And

Melanie was right. He did live to be old. He would die in 1924 at the age of eighty-two.

Melanie was still not happy in Diou. The lax and worldly life of the French and the lack of piety distressed her tremendously.

"I can't breathe here!" she said again and again. "The air is foul with sin. It is full of pestilence."

In the face of such unhappiness, the Abbé agreed that she could leave. As he was her spiritual director, she would not take such a step without his permission.

He suggested a final pilgrimage to La Salette. Melanie agreed to that very happily. So they set forth—to Grenoble by train, then from Grenoble to Corps by stagecoach.

Melanie remembered a similar trip many years ago, when Bishop Ginoulhiac was the Bishop of Grenoble. She was in the stagecoach talking with some pleasant ladies from that city when one said to her, "Did you know that the Shepherdess of La Salette is now crazy?"

"Are you sure?" asked Melanie gently.

"Oh, yes, very sure," the second lady said. "It was Bishop Ginoulhiac himself who told us."

After Melanie had left the stagecoach at Corps, another passenger said to the ladies, "That was the Shepherdess herself whom you were talking to." The good ladies were left in a state of confusion and embarrassment.

Melanie had not lost her mind, but Bishop Ginoulhiac's mind clouded over, and he died insane.

The Abbé Combe and Melanie planned to go to La Salette very quietly and inconspicuously. But somehow word got out, and Melanie was met in Corps by some of her many relatives, who whisked her off to stay with them.

The next day Melanie and the Abbé journeyed to La Salette and the site of the Apparition. This always gave Melanie great happiness. After that she stopped at the house of her old master, Baptiste Pra, in Ablandin. The son of Baptiste was in the house, very ill.

"Oh, I have been praying that you would come to see me before I died," he said from his bed. He held her hand while the tears streamed down his face.

The Abbé noticed with what respect and veneration all the people of the mountains and of Corps regarded Melanie. As she passed through the streets of Corps, they came out of their houses to watch, saying, "There goes the Child of the Blessed Virgin." This was the name she went by in her birthplace.

Melanie left France forever in June of 1904 and returned to Italy. She left her work table and Little Brother's chair with the Abbé Combe. He gave the little chair to the museum at La Salette, where it is today.

Monsignor Cecchini, the Bishop of Altamura, Italy, a small town in the province of Bari, welcomed Melanie gladly. Altamura was in the extreme south of Italy and was very primitive, having no running water and "no toilets, not even in the bishop's house," as Melanie wrote. But the people there did love God, and that was a great comfort to her. The air, while not pure, was at least cleaner than that of France, she said.

Bishop Cecchini arranged for Melanie to have a room with the Gianuzzi family. These were pious, well-born people who were delighted to have the Shepherdess of La Salette staying with them. She stayed with them for several weeks. But Melanie did not want even good, kindly people observing her life of penances and mortifications. So she found a very small apartment where she had what she dearly loved, solitude and privacy. There she lived very peacefully for six months.

One morning the neighbors noticed that the shutters of Melanie's window were still closed. The door of her apartment was forced open, and there she was found, dead, and fully dressed, lying on the floor, as she had predicted. Two neighbors said that on the night before they had heard beautiful singing of the *Tantum Ergo* in the French lady's apartment. They also heard the tinkle of a little bell such as is used when bringing Holy Viaticum to the dying. The good people of Altamura said that Melanie had been brought Holy Communion by Our Lord Himself.

Far away in France, the Abbé Rigaux, a friend of Melanie's and also a friend of the Abbé Combe, had had an amazing dream on the night of December 14, 1904. He dreamed that he had seen the Blessed Virgin, who looked like a young girl of ravishing beauty, bending toward a woman. The woman, whose back was toward him, was holding out her arms toward the Blessed Virgin. Above the woman's head was a magnificent crown, and from her head, rays of light streamed up toward Heaven. The woman was wearing a black jacket edged with velour. Melanie had a jacket like that.

The Abbé Rigaux woke up with a start. It was a little after midnight. He thought about his strange dream for a while, then he drifted off to sleep again. He dreamed the same dream again. But the crown above the woman was now resting on her head. And as he watched, the hands of the Blessed Virgin joined with the hands of the woman.

The Abbé Rigaux woke up and wept. It was five o'clock on a dark winter's morning. The Abbé went to Diou to see his friend, the Abbé Combe, a week later. He told him of his wonderful dream.

"I think the woman was Melanie," he said.

"It was," said Abbé Combe. "That was not a dream, it was a vision." He had just had word from Italy that Melanie had died on the night of December 14.

Melanie had endured contradictions, scorn, contempt and injuries. But she had had indomitable courage and tenacity to pass on to the world the message of Our Lady of La Salette. And at the end of her hard journey, there was a heavenly crown waiting for her.

BIBLIOGRAPHY

Combe, Abbé. *Dernières années de la Soeur Marie de la Croix, Bergère de La Salette [1899-1904]: Journal de l'Abbé Combe.* Saint Céneré: Éditions Saint Michel, 1967.

de Salmiech, Charles, m.s., ed. *La Salette 1847-1855—Journal d'une Institutrice, D'après l'oeuvre de Marie des Brûlais: "L'Écho de la Sainte Montagne."* Paris: Nouvelles Éditions Latines, 1969.

Gouin, Abbé. *Soeur Marie de la Croix, Bergère de la Salette, née Mélanie Calvat, Tertiaire de St. Dominique, Victime de Jésus.* St. Céneré: Édition St.-Michel, 1970.

Guilhot, Hyacinthe. *La Vraie Melanie de La Salette.* St. Céneré: Éditions St.-Michel, 1960.

Kennedy, Father John S. *Light on the Mountain: The Story of La Salette.* Garden City, NY: Image Books, 1956.

La Douceur, Emile. *The Vision of La Salette.* New York: Vantage Press, 1956.

Le Hidec, Max. *Les Secrets de La Salette.* Paris: Nouvelles Éditions Latines, 1969.

New Catholic Encyclopedia, Vol. XIV. New York: McGraw-Hill Book Co., 1967.

Pour Servir a l'Histoire Réelle de La Salette (documents), Vol. I, Vol. II, Vol. III. Paris: Nouvelles Éditions Latines, 1963, 1964.

Trochu, Abbé Francis. *The Curé D'Ars: St. Jean-Marie-Baptiste Vianney (1786-1859).* London: Burns Oates & Washbourne, 1927; Rockford, IL: TAN, 1977.

PRAYER TO THE HOLY TRINITY

To obtain the glorification of Its humble servant, Sister Mary of the Cross, Shepherdess of La Salette, née Melanie Calvat. Imprimatur: Fr. Albertus Lepidi, Ord. Praed., S.P.A. Mag., June 6, 1922, Rome.

O MOST BLESSED TRINITY, source of all sanctification, we offer Thee, through the gracious hands of Our Lady of La Salette, Reconciler of Sinners, our poor reparations for so many Satanic blasphemies, for the manifold profanations of Sundays and Holy Days of Obligation, and for the equally proud contempt for the absolute obligation of prayer, penance and mortification. Make all to know the greatness of Thy love for men, and to appreciate the heavenly treasures which give perfect renunciation of self and of the world and thus subordinate earthly things to the one thing necessary, eternal salvation.

These gifts were given to Melanie, the faithful messenger of the Queen of Heaven, and through her merits we beg them of Thee. Grant us her beloved virtues of humility, self-sacrifice and charity; and in order to manifest ever more fully her favor with Thine Infinite Majesty, grant through her intercession that our prayers, full of faith, trust and love, may obtain for us the favor of (*name your request*), while we submit ourselves to Thy Divine Will, whatever that may be. We thank Thee for all Thy benefits, spiritual and temporal, through which may we deserve to come and adore Thee in the eternal happiness of Heaven. Amen.

"May Jesus be loved by all hearts!"

Say three Paters, Aves and Glorias for the glory of the adorable Trinity and in honor of the Blessed Virgin Mary.

Please report all favors obtained, especially through novenas, to the

> Religieuses du Divin Zèle
> 144, Via Circonvallazione Appia
> 00179 Roma
> Italia

If you have enjoyed this book, consider making your next selection from among the following . . .

Prices guaranteed through June 30, 1997.

Miraculous Images of Our Lady. *Cruz* 20.00
Raised from the Dead. *Fr. Hebert* 15.00
Love and Service of God, Infinite Love. *Mother Louise Margaret* . 10.00
Life and Work of Mother Louise Margaret. *Fr. O'Connell* 10.00
Autobiography of St. Margaret Mary 4.00
Thoughts and Sayings of St. Margaret Mary 3.00
The Voice of the Saints. *Comp. by Francis Johnston* 5.00
The 12 Steps to Holiness and Salvation. *St. Alphonsus* 7.00
The Rosary and the Crisis of Faith. *Cirrincione & Nelson* 1.25
Sin and Its Consequences. *Cardinal Manning* 5.00
Fourfold Sovereignty of God. *Cardinal Manning* 5.00
Dialogue of St. Catherine of Siena. *Transl. Algar Thorold* 9.00
Catholic Answer to Jehovah's Witnesses. *D'Angelo* 8.00
Twelve Promises of the Sacred Heart. (100 cards) 5.00
Life of St. Aloysius Gonzaga. *Fr. Meschler* 10.00
The Love of Mary. *D. Roberto* 7.00
Begone Satan. *Fr. Vogl* 2.00
The Prophets and Our Times. *Fr. R. G. Culleton* 11.00
St. Therese, The Little Flower. *John Beevers* 4.50
St. Joseph of Copertino. *Fr. Angelo Pastrovicchi* 4.50
Mary, The Second Eve. *Cardinal Newman* 2.50
Devotion to Infant Jesus of Prague. *Booklet* .... .75
Reign of Christ the King in Public & Private Life. *Davies* 1.25
The Wonder of Guadalupe. *Francis Johnston* 6.00
Apologetics. *Msgr. Paul Glenn* 9.00
Baltimore Catechism No. 1 .... 3.00
Baltimore Catechism No. 2 .... 4.00
Baltimore Catechism No. 3 .... 7.00
An Explanation of the Baltimore Catechism. *Fr. Kinkead* 13.00
Bethlehem. *Fr. Faber* 16.50
Bible History. *Schuster* 10.00
Blessed Eucharist. *Fr. Mueller* 9.00
Catholic Catechism. *Fr. Faerber* 5.00
The Devil. *Fr. Delaporte* 5.00
Dogmatic Theology for the Laity. *Fr. Premm* 18.00
Evidence of Satan in the Modern World. *Cristiani* 8.50
Fifteen Promises of Mary. (100 cards) 5.00
Life of Anne Catherine Emmerich. 2 vols. *Schmoeger* 37.50
Life of the Blessed Virgin Mary. *Emmerich* 15.00
Manual of Practical Devotion to St. Joseph. *Patrignani* 13.50
Prayer to St. Michael. (100 leaflets) 5.00
Prayerbook of Favorite Litanies. *Fr. Hebert* 9.00
Preparation for Death. (Abridged). *St. Alphonsus* 7.00
Purgatory Explained. *Schouppe* 13.50
Purgatory Explained. (pocket, unabr.). *Schouppe* 7.50
Fundamentals of Catholic Dogma. *Ludwig Ott* 20.00
Spiritual Conferences. *Tauler* 12.00
Trustful Surrender to Divine Providence. *Bl. Claude* 4.00
Wife, Mother and Mystic. *Bessieres* 7.00
The Agony of Jesus. *Padre Pio* 1.50

Prices guaranteed through June 30, 1997.

At your Bookdealer or direct from the Publisher.

Prices guaranteed through June 30, 1997.

ABOUT THE AUTHOR

Mary Alice Dennis was born in Paris during World War I to a U.S. Marine officer and his devout Catholic wife. Her father's assignments took the family to many places far from home. Mary Alice would eventually attend 12 different schools in five countries. She learned French in a very strict convent boarding school in Paris at age 13—a fruitful year, but one which "almost killed" her, since she had been taught in a relaxed atmosphere with a three-hours-per-day correspondence course the previous year. She says the year at the convent gave her a great respect for French schooling and "got me through four years of Bryn Mawr College." Mary Alice Dennis' experiences in China from age 14-16 became the background for her adventure story published in 1975 entitled *The Young Griffins of Shanghai.* Her own ancestral background is largely Irish; in fact, her great-grandfather authored the popular song, "The Rose of Tralee." After graduating from Bryn Mawr, she spent an exciting two years with the Red Cross in France and England during the last part of World War II. Returning home to the United States in 1944, she married John Dennis. The couple have three children and several grandchildren. Some years ago Mrs. Dennis became intrigued by the remarkable childhood experiences of Melanie Calvat, one of the two seers at La Salette, France in 1846. This interest eventually led to the writing of *Melanie—And the Story of Our Lady of La Salette.* The author's husband has himself written a number of books on nature. The couple currently make their home in Maryland's Eastern Shore region.